The American Abraham

Cambridge Studies in American Literature and Culture

Editor
Albert Gelpi, Stanford University

Advisory Board
Nina Baym, University of Illinois, Champaign-Urbana
Sacvan Bercovitch, Harvard University
Richard Bridgman, University of California, Berkeley
David Levin, University of Virginia
Joel Porte, Harvard University
Mike Weaver, Oxford University

Other books in the series
Robert Zaller: *The Cliffs of Solitude*
Peter Conn: *The Divided Mind*
Patricia Caldwell: *The Puritan Conversion Narrative*
Stephen Fredman: *Poet's Prose*
Charles Altieri: *Self and Sensibility in Contemporary American Poetry*
John McWilliams, Jr.: *Hawthorne, Melville, and the American Character*
Barton St. Armand: *Emily Dickinson and Her Culture*
Elizabeth McKinsey: *Niagara Falls*
Mitchell Robert Breitwieser: *Cotton Mather and Benjamin Franklin*
Albert J. von Frank: *The Sacred Game*
Marjorie Perloff: *The Dance of the Intellect*
Albert Gelpi: *Wallace Stevens*
Ann Kibbey: *The Interpretation of Material Shapes in Puritanism*
Sacvan Bercovitch and Myra Jehlen: *Ideology and Classic American Literature*
Karen Rowe: *Saint and Singer*
Lawrence Buell: *New England Literary Culture*
David Wyatt: *The Fall into Eden*
Paul Giles: *Hart Crane*
Steven Axelrod and Helen Deese: *Robert Lowell*
Jerome Loving: *Emily Dickinson*
Brenda Murphy: *American Realism and American Drama, 1880–1940*
George Dekker: *The American Historical Romance*
Richard Gray: *Writing the South*
Brook Thomas: *Cross-Examinations of Law and Literature*

The American Abraham

James Fenimore Cooper and the Frontier Patriarch

WARREN MOTLEY

Rutgers University

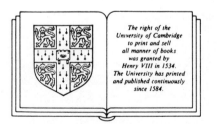

The right of the
University of Cambridge
to print and sell
all manner of books
was granted by
Henry VIII in 1534.
The University has printed
and published continuously
since 1584.

CAMBRIDGE UNIVERSITY PRESS

CAMBRIDGE

NEW YORK   NEW ROCHELLE   MELBOURNE   SYDNEY

Published by the Press Syndicate of the University of Cambridge
The Pitt Building, Trumpington Street, Cambridge CB2 1RP
32 East 57th Street, New York, NY 10022, USA
10 Stamford Road, Oakleigh, Melbourne 3166, Australia

First published 1987

Printed in the United States of America

Library of Congress Cataloging-in-Publication Data
Motley, Warren.
The American Abraham.
(Cambridge studies in American literature and
culture)
Bibliography: p.
Includes index.
1. Cooper, James Fenimore, 1789–1851 – Political
and social views. 2. Patriarchy in literature.
3. Authority in literature. 4. Family in literature.
5. Fathers in literature. 6. Frontier and pioneer life
in literature. I. Title. II. Series.
PS1442.P38M6   1987   813'.2   86–33358

British Library Cataloguing in Publication Data
Motley, Warren
The American Abraham: James Fenimore Cooper
and the frontier patriarch. – (Cambridge
studies in American literature and culture)
1. Cooper, James Fenimore – Criticism
and interpretation
I. Title
813'.2   PS1438

ISBN 0 521 32782 2

*To Matthew and William
and to Cynthia*

Contents

vii

Acknowledgments

No matter how direct a narrative the critic finally charts, the route to discover a clear line of argument is likely to be an odyssey of intellectual twists and turns. To those guides who have come to me in the shape both of Mentor and of Athena, I owe the completion of this particular journey.

At Rutgers, I have been buoyed by the energy and loyalty of extraordinary colleagues. For their generosity and sustaining counsel, I thank them all, and especially Alice Crozier, Marianne DeKoven, Elissa Greenwald, William Keach, David Leverenz, Richard Poirier, Barry Qualls, Arnold Rampersad, Elaine Showalter, Catharine Stimpson, and Thomas Van Laan. Nor would I have retained my sense of critical perspective or humor without the cadre of Americanists and adopted Americanists who laughed and debated in the labyrinthine corridors of the English Department. Beyond Rutgers I owe special thanks for the encouragement and insight of Sharon O'Brien and Richard Yarborough.

Without the example of George Dekker and Albert Gelpi, I cannot imagine my life as a scholar and teacher. With unstinting helpfulness, George Dekker queried and strengthened countless drafts of the broader work on frontier literature from which this book took its start. Later in the voyage, when writing seemed the most solitary of trials, Albert Gelpi read, listened, and spoke the essential word of advice – "onward." Whatever I have been able to offer my own students has been the reflection of deep

ix

gratitude for the generosity of these men and of my other teachers at Stanford and Harvard.

I wrote much of this book in a Brooklyn storefront, the unused half of a neighborhood luggage store: "Spedizioni – Prelievi Bagaglio." To my friends outside academia who made writing a way of joining a community, not a prescription for isolation from it, I owe an unpayable debt. I also want to thank Rutgers University for the economic support that made a crucial semester of steady writing possible.

Without James Franklin Beard's superb editing of *The Letters and Journals of James Fenimore Cooper*, work on the interplay of the novelist's life and art could barely begin. In addition to the many intellectual debts I have acknowledged within the text, special thanks must go to this pioneer.

Writing a critical study is part and parcel of one's life – sometimes too large and unwieldy a parcel. I thank my wife, Cynthia Saltzman, for her enabling encouragement and understanding. Informing this book at all levels is what I have learned from her, from my parents and siblings, from the larger family that has taught me since childhood, and now from my own two children. I am happy to have reality speak to me in the clear tones of a dawn-rising three-year-old who takes less stock in books than in breakfast — "Wake up. I am very starving."

Introduction

The literature of frontier settlement is dominated not by the
solitary woodsman in the tradition of Natty Bumppo but by
the pioneer patriarch – the American Abraham – who leaves
the society of his forefathers to establish his family in the wilderness. Like the famous *isolatoes* of our literature, the American
Abraham strikes out for the West, but for him the migration is
strategic rather than an essential part of his being. Whereas Natty
feels a centrifugal pressure repeatedly impelling him to a distant
orbit, the patriarch is driven by the centripetal impulse of his
own will to seize authority at the center. While Natty and his
successors live alone, in the open air, in a Concord cabin, in an
iron cot in Yoknapatawpha County, the patriarch must group
people around him and bind them to his vision in order to feel
his destiny – at Templeton, at Rancho de los Muertos, at Sutpen's Hundred.

In general, James Fenimore Cooper's romances of frontier
settlement pass over the earliest intrusions of white civilization
into the wilderness, made by hunters and military men, to focus
instead on the first communities, their growth, and their gradual
reabsorption into the national or colonial culture from which
the patriarch and his followers had originally ventured. In that
"intermediate space," Crèvecoeur had proposed, an observer
"might contemplate the very beginning and outlines of human
society, which can be traced nowhere now but in this part of
the world" (12). If for a moment we accept Edwin Fussell's
proposal that the hero of the Leatherstocking tales represents

"America as it ought to be," then the frontier patriarch and his settlement represent a social experiment in which Cooper assesses different balances of authority and freedom that might enable American society actually to realize and perpetuate its possibilities.

Over the course of his career, Cooper returned to tales of patriarchal settlement more often even than to the wilderness of the Leatherstocking tales. When conjoined with romances of the Revolution and the sea – all dominated by the issue of patriarchal authority – the settlement novels gain still more prominence. Although they lack a single unifying character like the Leatherstocking, their thematic cohesion and their common focus on recurring representations of the American Abraham properly give them the character of a series. Over the course of Cooper's career, he moved from one series to the next in fairly regular swings across a point of equilibrium imaginatively charted by the tensions contained within *The Pioneers* and *The Prairie* – the two romances claimed by both series. From *The Pioneers* (1823) he moved into the darker wilderness of *The Last of the Mohicans* (1826); after renewing his study of the patriarch in *The Prairie* (1827), he devoted himself fully to it in *The Wept of Wish-Ton-Wish* (1829). On his return from Europe he revived Natty Bumppo in *The Pathfinder* (1840) and *The Deerslayer* (1841). He then closely paralleled *The Wept* in *Wyandotté* (1843) before extending his interest in frontier settlement into the four-generation family chronicle of *The Littlepage Manuscripts,* including *Satanstoe* (1845), *The Chainbearer* (1845), and *The Redskins* (1846). As the concluding romance of the patriarchal series, *The Crater* (1847) reveals the strong psychic connection between the two series – between isolato[1] and patriarch.

Examining the issue of authority from the earliest years of Cooper's career to near its close, the tales of frontier settlement offer insights into the relationship between Cooper's art and his evolving position in family and society. In *The Protestant Temperament,* a study of American families over two centuries, Philip Greven argues that a person's response to political and religious authority in society is influenced in predictable ways by his or her adaptation to authority within the family – that an adult's trust or distrust of civil authority is influenced by the particular

mixture of authority and affection shown by his or her father
during childhood. Although Greven's particular categorization
of familial styles and his assertion of their continuity beyond
the usual bounds of historical periods have been considered
controversial, his central premise remains of essential importance
to the study of families in literary works. In Cooper's case, the
familial images within the novels of frontier settlement serve to
negotiate between the powerful childhood presence of Cooper's
father and issues of social and political authority he faced as an
adult. In thinking of literary works as a form of imaginative
negotiation with authority, I have tried to look beyond childhood sources of identity and to avoid a static view of Cooper's
psyche. This study stresses the ideas that a person's role within
the family changes with age and that these changes, in turn,
establish altered alignments with the parental figures of the psyche. I have tried to keep before myself and my readers a sense
of an evolving progression from Cooper's childhood dependence
on a father of unquestioned patriarchal stature, to his own assumption of paternal authority as a husband and father, to his
claims of authority over the American reading public, and finally
to his frustrations at the loss of public authority at the end of
his career.[2] In this sense, the history of Cooper's frontier patriarchs delineates the interaction of his life and art.

Cooper and writers following him seized on the intersecting
images of patriarchal family and frontier because of their extraordinary synecdochic power in our culture.[3] The metaphor
of the patriarchal family and its Lockean modifications per-
meated political and educational theory as well as partisan rhetoric during the Revolutionary and Constitutional debates and
those leading to the Civil War. To a writer of fiction, the interplay of family and society offered a ready-made metaphor.
It had been secured in the minds of readers as a principal ana-
logical pathway between private and public experience.[4]

Early New England societies depended on the premise that
political and ecclesiastical authority derived from the authority
of the father over his family; the family was in fact the "very
First Society that by the Direction and Providence of GOD is produced among the Children of Men" (Mather, *Family Religion
Urged* 1). The Puritans themselves called attention to the "Me-

taphoric and Synecdochical usage of the words *Father* and *Moth-er*"; John Cotton's catechism trained children to understand the Father and Mother of the Fifth Commandment as "All our Su-periours, whether in Family, School, Church, and Common-wealth" (Morgan 46, 19). And despite differences between dis-senters and cavaliers, the founders of the southern colonies shared the same assumptions. The family's place in political theory as the "first and most natural development of the social nature" went back at least to Aristotle, but the connection be-tween family and society was not perceived as something set in the anthropological past (Woodward xxxiv). Families not only made up the "foundation of all societies"; they continued to shape the present in their role as the "Nurseries of all Societies" (Morgan 143). The persistent convictions that circumstances within the family projected themselves into society and that the order of society reciprocally imprinted itself on the family un-derlay the synecdochic usefulness of the frontier settlement.

By focusing on the patriarchal family, Cooper joined the es-sential methodological insight of Alexis de Tocqueville to the literary paradigms of historical investigation he found in Sir Walter Scott.[5] Tocqueville's ultimate value as an observer of America depended less on his acumen as an observer – his data were too scanty for that – than on his theoretical insight into the relationship between a nation's politics and its social con-ditions. Setting out his plan for *Democracy in America,* Tocque-ville argued that while a nation's social condition is commonly thought of as the result of political and economic "circumstan-ces," once a social condition is established, it "may justly be considered as itself the source of almost all the laws, the usages, and the ideas which regulate the conduct of nations: whatever it does not produce, it modifies" (I: 46). Tocqueville drew this lesson from Napoleon's unsuccessful effort to placate Europeans with civil reforms; he had been hoisted by the petard of his own Napoleonic codes. They had made his overthrow inevitable, "for in the end political institutions never fail to become the image and expression of civil society, and in this sense it may be said that nothing is more political in a nation than its civil legislation" (II: 193). When he moved from theory to specifics,

Tocqueville, like Cooper, focused on the family: to him, the laws of inheritance – in other words, those laws that treat the family as the basic economic unit of society – should "be placed at the head of all political institutions; for they exercise an incredible influence upon the social state of a people" (I: 47). Crèvecoeur, too, directed his readers to the continuity between generations, although, like Locke and Rousseau, he placed more emphasis on education than on economics: "The easiest way of becoming acquainted with the modes of thinking, the rules of conduct, and the prevailing manners of any people, is to examine what sort of education they give their children, how they treat them at home, and what they are taught in their places of public worship" (113).[6]

When Cooper placed a patriarchal family on the frontier, he raised the metaphoric ante even higher. As Edwin Fussell and Henry Nash Smith have shown, the frontier was the expressive emblem of dialectical tensions between the Old World and the New, past and future, order and liberty – the list goes on – surrounding the invention of a new culture. Novels in which the frontier provides scenario and setting as well as metaphor let writers test, in an almost experimental way, the cohesive or divisive effects of specific social values from one generation to the next.

My first chapter lays out the paradigmatic tensions in Cooper's ideas about authority by analyzing a work placed at the center of his career, *The Wept of Wish-Ton-Wish*. This romance marks an important hiatus between the anxieties of a prolonged effort to establish his familial and professional authority and the bitterness of his later career, when the American public increasingly turned away from him. The second chapter circles back to the decade immediately preceding Cooper's decision to become a writer and investigates the origins of Cooper's compulsion to meet, over and over again, the issue of authority. Chapter 3 examines how Cooper's prose style is implicated in his efforts to negotiate with superior male figures, first by looking at the early letters of his childhood and adolescence and then by charting the shifting stylistic strategies he exploited in *The Pioneers* to bring the remarkable history of his father's frontier enterprises under the control of his art. Chapter 4 explores the darker vision of *The Prairie,* where, fortified by a string of literary successes, Cooper faced his deepest fears of the patriarch's filicidal threat.

Chapter 5 moves forward again to the later years of Cooper's career. One of the loveliest and most relaxed of Cooper's books, *Satanstoe* investigates the origins of American independence, but it proposes a much less radical version of change than had earlier works like *The Spy.* Disturbed by the sense of personal and political dislocation he felt in common with other American writers during the 1830s and 1840s, Cooper drew an alternative to the patriarchal paradigm. He set forth a model of familial and social development that would reconcile son and father, past and future, tradition and change. The final chapter documents the opposed impulses that met in Cooper's later romances. *The Crater* strains between Cooper's desire to analyze and influence the American scene and his longing to retreat into the more embracing world he preferred to imagine.

This study begins at the center of Cooper's career because in *The Wept of Wish-Ton-Wish* Cooper released the full archetypal power of his frontier paradigm by invoking the story of Abraham. The parallels between pioneer and Biblical founder were deeply rooted in Cooper's sources (Beale vii; Dekker, "Hadley" 219). In the *Magnalia Christi Americana,* Cotton Mather reported that the early settlers habitually invoked the story of Abraham, particularly at moments of crisis in their migration. To quiet their anxieties about leaving Leyden and Europe behind them, the founders of Plymouth had to satisfy themselves that "they had as plain a command of Heaven to attempt a removal, as ever their father Abraham had for his leaving the Caldean territories" (48). Similarly, the founders of Massachusetts Bay, arriving "at Salem, in the year 1629, resolved, like their father Abraham, to begin their plantation with calling on the name of the Lord" (70). The idea that patriarchal authority extended out from the family to society at large originated in the Puritan doctrine that God's covenant with Abraham extended to his entire household: "The germ of all political and ecclesiastical authority" lay in this duty, inherited from Abraham, to reform good behavior in the family (Morgan 135). When Mark Heathcote prays over the still-smoldering embers of his settlement and compares himself directly to "Abraham of old," he announces his self-conscious place in the Puritan tradition (240).[7]

By emphasizing the parallels between his patriarch and Abraham, Cooper endowed his story with the purpose and scale of an epic. As Abraham was a representative hero of the Judeo-Christian tradition, so Cooper's Puritan patriarch exemplified the underlying values of the new American culture taking its westward way. This deliberate parallel set the stakes high. The conflict between tendencies toward order and toward disorder within the westward impulse became a battle between light and darkness over a paradise, regained or once more lost. Even in those works, such as *The Prairie* and *The Chainbearer,* that concentrate on the antisocial aspects of the patriarchal venture, the sense of epic scale persists. Ishmael Bush and Aaron Timberman may be outcasts and false prophets of freedom, but they claim the stature of their Old Testament names.

To the nineteenth-century observer, the rapidity of the westward exodus and its awesome force seemed to make historical forces visible and brought them to the public's consciousness, in much the same way that Napoleon's conquests, or so Lukács argued, brought a sense of history to ordinary Europeans earlier in the century. Though not often given to contemplations of the Almighty, Tocqueville felt an epic impulse when he witnessed the migration's force: "The gradual and continuous progress of the European race towards the Rocky Mountains has the solemnity of a providential event; it is like a deluge of men rising unabatedly, and daily driven onwards by the hand of God" (I: 398). Tocqueville acknowledges not only the deluge's destructiveness to the native population but its power over Europeans as well. His use of the passive "driven" captures the evolving nineteenth-century feeling that these historical forces had never been controlled even by those who profited by them. For Americans, the epic images of the frontier prefigure later images of controlling forces projected by turn-of-the-century naturalists.

To Cooper, Abraham's story offered a mythic typology of generational conflict and historical change. Although Cooper avoided exact parallels to the Biblical text even in *The Wept of Wish-Ton-Wish,* two determining episodes in Abraham's life underlie his evaluations of the frontier patriarch. The first is Abraham's decision to go out from his father's house, leaving the land of his forefathers; the second is his acquiescence in sacrificing Isaac at the Lord's command. At both crises, Abraham's obedience to God is tested against his allegiance to human history – to its past, represented by the father, and to its future, represented by the son. Is an abrupt break with the past desirable or even possible? Does movement imply change, or merely repetition? Does the voice commanding the patriarch have divine sanction, or is it the delusory projection of his own will? Does the rebellion of one generation liberate or enslave the next? These are the questions Abraham's story poses as it takes on archetypal significance in Cooper's work.

I

Paradigmatic Tensions:
The American Abraham and
The Wept of Wish-Ton-Wish

As the first romance of frontier settlement outside the Leatherstocking series, *The Wept of Wish-Ton-Wish* (1829) offers a number of important advantages as a starting point. Cooper's portrait of Mark Heathcote is among his most balanced studies of the patriarch. By adopting a tone at once ironic and respectful, Cooper questions Heathcote's pride and inflexibility without denying his courage, decisiveness, and devotion. He persuades us that the patriarch's virtues and flaws flow from identical qualities of mind and that the migration into the wilderness is prompted by nobility and self-delusion alike. As a result of Cooper's balanced view, the form of *The Wept,* with its parallel examinations of Heathcote's relation to the past and future, is as nearly paradigmatic as that of any study of the American Abraham.

The sense of balance in *The Wept of Wish-Ton-Wish* seems to reflect its poised position at a key turning point in Cooper's professional and personal development. He began work on *The Wept* at the height of his success, confident of his position as the nation's leading novelist (Beard xxxix). In the eight years since the publication of *The Spy* in 1821, Cooper had produced a second romance of the Revolution, two sea tales, three volumes of the Leatherstocking tales, and a major nonfiction account of American political and social life. His economic success had at last released him from a grinding effort to disentangle himself from debt and allowed him to take his family to Europe. His distance from the American scene in general and the obligations of his extensive family connections in particular further contributed to the equilibrium of *The Wept*. The romance's paradigmatic balance offers an accessible entry into the informing tensions of Cooper's art during that relatively short period of suspension and calm between his departure in 1826 from the United States under John Quincy Adams and his return in 1833 as an older man to a changed Jacksonian America.

The intertwined respect and skepticism toward the patriarch of Wept-Ton-Wish provides an essential clue to Cooper's imaginative alternation between heroes like Heathcote, Judge Temple, and Herman Mordaunt, praised when they exert patriarchal control over a society tending always toward fragmentation, and heroes like Natty Bumppo, identified by his refusal to submit to outside authority and by his successive breaks from society. Though Cooper's ambivalence toward authority carries his oeuvre through unusually wide arcs, it also uncovers Cooper's true representativeness as a member of what historians term the second-generation cohort. In his ambivalence toward authority, he takes his place not only among writers like Emerson, Hawthorne, and Melville but among central political figures like Jackson and Lincoln as well. When we see his career whole, extending from the 1820s to mid-century, from Irving's *Sketch-Book* to *The Scarlet Letter,* from the Missouri Compromise to the rending debates over the Fugitive Slave Laws, Cooper seems less a predecessor than a peer, insistent on achieving independence as a rebellious son, and on being acknowledged in his own right as a father of his nation's literature.

Of Cooper's frontier romances, *The Wept of Wish-Ton-Wish* also looks furthest back into American history. Immersing himself in seventeenth- and eighteenth-century histories, Cooper traced the western migration to its origins in a Puritan era dominated by its synecdochic understanding of family, church, and state. Throughout Cooper's fiction, the pioneers tearing up the wilderness in their trek across New York State – the Billy Kirbys, Hurry Harry Marches, Aaron Timbermans, and Joel Strides – rise like spring rocks from New England soil. Convinced that this energetic horde would dominate the nation's emerging culture, Cooper viewed the invaders with suspicion. Tocqueville's observation only a few years later that thirty-one new members of Congress from the trans-Appalachian states had been born in Connecticut – the setting of *The Wept* – would hardly have quieted Cooper's New Anglophobia. In *The Wept* Cooper explores those qualities of the Puritan mind that led men west and that also led a stern theology held by admirable men of considerable stature to degenerate into the selfishness and rapacity exhibited by later pioneers. On the other hand, Cooper found in the patriarchal authority wielded by the founders of New England an antidote to social fragmentation. In Puritan communality, he saw qualities needed to reassert an organic connection between the individual and society.

In its plot, *The Wept of Wish-Ton-Wish* offers a particularly clear example of the structure underlying Cooper's tales of frontier settlement from *The Pioneers* to *The Crater*. Typically, these works trace the community's development through two phases. In the first, a father leads his family and retainers to an isolated landholding in the wilderness. During the initial stage of its development, the community is cut off from the civilized world and depends largely on the leadership of the founding patriarch. It prospers or falters in accordance with his energy, moral stature, and social vision. The romances then describe a second phase, when the increasing power of new immigrants and the settlement's incorporation into the economic and political system of the colony or state reduce the authority of the original patriarch.

In *The Wept*, Mark Heathcote takes his family from the relative security of the Massachusetts Bay Colony and exposes them to the dangers of the Connecticut wilderness in the 1660s. The first half of the romance outlines the patriarch's efforts to transform the valley into a habitable garden, to maintain independence from the colonial government, and to live in the wilderness among the aborigines without violation of either. His settlement comes to a sudden end, however, when an Indian attack reduces the theocratic utopia to ashes. Though all seems lost, the second half reveals that the settlers saved themselves by a strategic retreat into a tunnel. Improbable as this might seem, both the unlooked-for extinction and the unlikely salvation have crucial significance in Cooper's psychic world picture. In the later chapters, Cooper follows two thematic lines:

the decline of the settlement's leadership and the barriers against accommodating Europeans and native Americans. A decade after the settlement's reemergence, civil, military, and religious authority has been divided among a group of unimpressive men who join the colony's genocidal campaign against the Indians. In order to underscore the declining standards of the patriarch's followers, the second half closely parallels the first. In each, the action turns on a climactic Indian attack and a child's captivity by the opposite racial group; the moral issues raised by European conquest are framed by debates over vengeance and the possibility of racial adaptation (McWilliams 248; Ringe, *The Pictorial Mode* 157–62).

The pioneer's willingness to cut himself off from the past so troubled Cooper that he transformed Abraham's *obedience* into Heathcote's *desertion*. Where the Bible, taking God's point of view, affirms Abraham's departure from the ancestral land, Cooper felt that Heathcote and his fellow Puritans, having "deserted the fire-sides of their forefathers," were guilty of betrayal (15). Throughout his work, Cooper assigned special significance to the paternal hearth as a radiant source of security, happiness, refinement, and moral enlightenment. Protecting that hearth, the father's stronghold dominated Cooper's highly structured settings. As H. Daniel Peck observes, Cooper often organized his landscapes around a symbolic prominence, whether a jutting cliff in the forest or an island in the Pacific, that served as a moral center of gravity holding the action within the limited perimeter so important to historical fiction (91). Though Cooper halfheartedly covered his tracks by claiming such imaginary topographies were "natural," he often conceded, as he did in *The Wept,* that the sharp rise in the land had "the appearance of a work of art" (26). Crowning these elevations stood the patriarch's fortified house. Within its walls, and often within a still more hallowed chamber at its center, civilized life continued at the fireside. And there, protected both by the paternal elevation and the more maternal, womblike shelter of the inner sanctum, the household worshiped, received worldly and spiritual instruction, and discussed the problems of governance. There too, at least in temples less austere than Heathcote's, men and women warmed themselves with the pleasures of Madeira, tobacco, and good talk. In manners as well as morals lay the preservation of the world. In short, standards were upheld to give order and value to the surrounding, often benighted, scene. To Cooper, the patriarch's fireside represented security and tradition in the midst of danger and change.

Particularly in Cooper's later work, the fireside demanded vigilant protection. In the surrounding society, greed, selfishness, and envy always threatened. Cooper was keenly aware of the human capacity for violence. His father had been murdered by a blow from behind delivered without warning, and Cooper never lost his sense of how swiftly the vestments of civilization could fall to reveal the naked natural brute. In the Leatherstocking tales, violence lurks behind every tree; in the social novels it lies behind every political disruption. Like one of the islands in *The Crater,* society always seemed to him a habitable volcano – dormant, but not extinct. The slightest seismic tremor through society might erupt into demagoguery and political chaos.

In his concern that breaking from the restraints of established culture would unleash violence, Cooper invoked one of the most prolonged debates raised by the discovery of the New World. Enlightenment thinkers asked whether colonists would realize the bounty of the New World or whether, freed from social restraint, they would degenerate morally to the level of the savages indigenous to the wilderness. Like many debates of the eighteenth century, it began as a question among natural scientists over botanical and zoological classification and grew into a philosophical controversy over human nature. The most famous American contribution was Jefferson's *Notes on the State of Virginia* (1785). In classic encyclopedic style, Jefferson sought to counter the great French naturalist Buffon and his assertion that men as well as plants and animals had succumbed to the inferior climate of America. Buffon asserted that nature in America was not a kind mother, but a "marâtre," a wicked stepmother who refused to nurture her children. Abbé Raynal extended the theory of degeneracy from the indigenous people and maintained that signs of physical degeneracy would become apparent in Europeans transplanted to America.[1]

Even in the course of his rebuttal, Jefferson expressed concern

that men on the farthest frontiers had, in fact, declined to a
semibarbarous moral state. At one point, he suggests that white
men living in the wild may have sunk to a state of greater sav-
agery than those indigenous tribes living by a strict, though
primitive, morality. As a loyalist who lost everything during
the Revolution, Crèvecoeur brought forward evidence to confirm this anxiety more readily than did Jefferson. With Cooper,
Crèvecoeur was one of the few writers whom Americans heard
voicing the shadow side of the Revolution. Crèvecoeur made
the botanical vocabulary of the Enlightenment debate a governing metaphor of the *Letters*. He constantly referred to men
as plants and looked to see what made them flourish or falter
when transplanted to the New World. When he looked at men
who marched farthest into the wilderness, he observed that "it
is with men as it is with plants and animals that grow and live
in the forests; they are entirely different from those that live in
the plains" (51). And he tells the difference darkly. The motives
of these pioneers are various; they have been "driven there by
misfortunes, necessity of beginnings, desire for acquiring large
tracts of land, idleness, frequent want of economy, ancient
debts" (46). Sometimes they are moved by society's failure, but
more often by their own. In all cases, their motives are individual
rather than collective. Crèvecoeur acknowledged that "the re-
union of such people does not afford a very pleasing spectacle"
(46). Like Cooper, he ascribed the "contention, inactivity, and
wretchedness" that often ensued to insufficient checks on human
nature (46). These evils exist everywhere, but in the wilderness
"there are not the same remedies . . . as in a long established
community" (46). Lacking qualified magistrates, men exist
"often in a perfect state of war" (46). Men are "wholly left dependent on their native tempers, and on the spur of uncertain
industry, which often fails when not sanctified by the efficacy
of a few moral rules. There, remote from the power of example
and check of shame, many families exhibit the most hideous
part of our society" (47).

In the early letters, Crèvecoeur was able to deal with the
prospect with equanimity, as Cooper could in *The Pioneers*. He
saw these forest creatures as "a kind of forlorn hope": the "im-
pure part serves as our precursors or pioneers" without cor-

rupting the whole (47). Just behind these pioneers lay the communities that redeem Europeans by that power of transplantation (47). But when war lifted the controls of morality, the violence of the far frontier swept back over the pastoral communities Crèvecoeur celebrated. Neighbors who had joined in raising each other's houses – for Crèvecoeur the symbolic act of joining individual to community – regressed to a "state of war" and razed those houses to the ground (46, 198–231).

Since Cooper was generally less sanguine than Crèvecoeur about society's hold on man, we can understand why he found Heathcote's decision dangerous when he set the "Father of the universe" in opposition to his earthly "forefathers." Religion and tradition, Cooper believed, must be kept united or their tenuous hold over man would be usurped by the destructive forces in his fallen nature. "The first direct mandates of God, as delivered on Mount Sinai," he wrote in *The American Democrat*, "were to impress the Jews with a sense of their duties to their heavenly Father; the next to impress them with the first of their social duties, that of honor and obedience to their parents" (80). While Cooper admired Heathcote's assertion of this commandment within his community, he assailed his self-proclaimed exemption from it in dealing with political authorities over him.

Cooper emphasized the threat inherent in Heathcote's decision to abandon his father's house by associating his migration with the English Civil War and then by steadily developing a more general link between frontier and revolution. As a young man, Mark Heathcote was among the "many men of deep and sincere piety" who took up arms against the Stuarts (13). Believing, however, that to seek worldly power was to risk spiritual corruption, Heathcote determined that exile was a wiser course than rebellion and departed for New England before the Puritan leadership executed Charles I. To clinch the correspondence, Cooper established a personal link between Heathcote and Cromwell:

> . . . and once, when commenting after evening prayer on the vanity and vicissitudes of this life, he acknowledged that the extraordinary individual, who was, in substance if not in name, seated on the throne of the Plantagenets, had been the boon

> companion and ungodly associate of many of his youthful
> hours. Then would follow a long, wholesome, extempora-
> neous homily on the idleness of setting the affections on the
> things of life, and a half-suppressed, but still intelligible com-
> mendation of the wiser course which led him to raise his own
> tabernacle in the wilderness. (21)

Declaring Heathcote and the Lord Protector boon companions
and ungodly associates, Cooper increases the stature of the fictional patriarch while underlining the similarity of exile and
rebel. Both men carry the spirit of dissent into action. When
they feel that conformity threatens personal salvation, they break
with society, denying its sovereignty and forfeiting its benefits.
Although the voyage to America seems at first to avoid violence
and the moral dangers of worldly power, it betrays the same
antagonism toward established social order as does civil war.
If, in England, the Puritan mind showed itself in revolution, in
America, Cooper proposed, it came forward in an ultimately
more enduring historic upheaval: the migration of Europeans
into the North American wilderness.

By linking frontier and revolution, Cooper synthesizes two
major symbols of the American experiment. As the Revolution
marked our military and political independence, so the frontier
became the primary metaphor of our cultural independence, of
the transformation of European mores into American ones. Together, the two symbols represent the birth of a nation, and
together they unite the anxieties aroused by the labor of that
birth.

To Cooper's audience in the 1820s, the idea of civil war would
still have resonated with the anxieties of our War of Independence and the rhetoric of shattered bonds between father and
son (Jenson 48; Fliegelman 67–122, 155–94). Though Cooper
shared, at times, the antipatriarchal call of Emerson's "Self-Re-
liance" to throw off the corpse of memory and to push further
the Revolution's rejection of the old order, at other moments
he shared a more conservative fear that the Revolution had re-
moved too much control. As Wendy Martin suggests, John
Adams betrayed his early sense that the Revolution might gain
too much momentum when he responded defensively to his
wife's challenge to remember the ladies (332). That concern with

loss of control, informing the conservative side of the American political spectrum from *The Federalist Papers* on, reveals itself in Cooper's uneasy accounts of the Revolution.

Hoping to support the liberal cause of General Lafayette with his publication of *Notions of the Americans* – in the months immediately preceding his work on *The Wept* – Cooper maneuvered, not altogether convincingly, to hide his discomfort with the idea of revolution. As Mike Ewart notes, to minimize the violence of the American Revolution, Cooper went so far as to assert that "Americans had no revolution, strictly speaking, they have only preceded the rest of Christendom in their reforms because circumstances permitted it" (Ewart 70; *Notions*, II, 339). This would have been news to readers of *The Spy* (1821). Cooper's fictional account of the war, his first successful novel, retains its ability to shock our childhood acceptance of a glorious revolution. It exposed greed and rapacity as the determining forces in the disputed neutral ground. Replacing the myth of villainous Redcoats and heroic patriots, Cooper imagined a battlefield world so pervasively gray that even a hero of Washington's stature avoids contamination only with the greatest difficulty.

Throughout *The Wept of Wish-Ton-Wish,* Cooper maintained the association between Heathcote and the English Civil War – between frontier and revolution – by linking Heathcote to a shadow figure based, like Sir Walter Scott's legend in *Peveril of the Peak* (1822) and Hawthorne's later "The Gray Champion" (1835), on the Angel of Hadley episode: New England legend recounted the mysterious appearance of an ancient Puritan who rescued the Massachusetts town from attack during King Philip's War. Early American chroniclers identified the figure with Generals Goffe and Whalley, regicide judges of Charles I (Dekker, "The Angel of Hadley"). The only other character of Heathcote's age and stature, the stranger, known only as Submission, lives in a symbiotic relationship with the patriarch's family. They nurture him and guard his secret; he warns them of approaching danger and directs their two defenses against the Indians. To a greater extent than either Scott's account or Hawthorne's, *The Wept* stresses the shadow figure's history as a regicide. Once companions in arms, Heathcote and the stranger took different courses. The latter, like Cromwell, stayed and took action against the king; Heathcote departed to avoid burdening his conscience with the consequences of pitting his Father in Heaven against his royal father. But their fates remain unmistakably intertwined. In hiding, Submission lives sequestered in a tower others know as Heathcote's religious retreat; when a visitor returns to the valley a century later, he discovers the graves of the two Puritans side by side.

In keeping with Cooper's balanced tone and divided sympathies, the unusual name of Submission pays tribute to his fortitude in exile and his stoic humility before God, but also comments ironically on his crime and on his life as a fugitive carrying two horse pistols at his side and a knife and pistol beneath his doublet. His life has become a relentless refusal to submit to authority. Cooper took the term "submission" from Cotton Mather, for whom it was a keystone of Puritan religious values; Mather used the term to praise the endurance of New Englanders during their first winter. It was first "their profound submission to the will of God" that "carried them cheerfully through the sorrows of this *mortality*" – sorrows brought on by the death of half the men in the camp (*Magnalia* 54). The tension between the admirable connotations of submission and the confusion of self-will with Providential will inherent in the ironic naming of the regicide allowed Cooper to show how abstract terms can shift almost unnoticeably from positive to negative connotations. By the time the second generation of rulers takes over the valley, they use the term with open hypocrisy to justify a ruthless and convenient decision to murder the Indian husband of Heathcote's granddaughter.

While submission is the term most representative of the theocracy's values, other key terms, more clearly applicable to Cooper's own time, seem always in danger of shifting ground. The most prominent of these is liberty. Cooper praises Heathcote as a man devoted to liberty without revolution. Yet, a moment later, he admits that a noticeable gleam comes into the leader's eye when he recounts his military prowess. The "leaning to liberty" may easily slip into the service of an instinctive lust for violence (20). The slippage is inherent in the word itself. As

a political ideal, liberty is an "exemption or freedom from arbitrary, despotic, or autocratic rule or control" (*OED*, 1961).
But as Cooper observed in *The Wept* and in later novels more
openly treating of contemporary politics, liberty in this sense
can easily slide toward its more individual, less communal definition as "the condition of being able to act in any desired way
without hindrance or restraint; faculty or power to do what one
likes." Once liberty sanctions individual volition rather than
political guarantees, the descent is rapid to the wholly negative
connotation of "license." Thus, within a word hailed as an in-
alienable right and a political cornerstone – the statue glints toward Brooklyn today – lies latent a possibility that would des-
ecrate the nobility of the abstraction.

Cooper believed that the revolutionary nature of the pioneers'
motives introduced a historical irony that persisted in his own
era: New England society was founded on an essentially antisocial principle. The strong impulse toward social conformity
and community enforcement so prominent in New England
counteracted a less visible but threatening tendency toward
fragmentation. If community authority opposed the command
of conscience, citizens could, as a final alternative, dissolve their
association with society by rebellion or exodus. In America, the
existence of apparently limitless land invited dissenters to choose
the latter alternative. Cooper believed that a society founded by
men in obedience to the private commands of conscience was
liable to dissolution by the same principle that created it: a society
of dissenters would be divided by dissent:

> . . . come from what quarter they might, schisms and doc-
> trinal contentions arose among the emigrants themselves; and
> men, who together had deserted the firesides of their fore-
> fathers in quest of religious peace, were ere long seen sepa-
> rating their fortunes, in order that each might enjoy, un-
> molested, those peculiar shades of faith, which all had the
> presumption no less than the folly, to believe were necessary
> to propitiate the omnipotent and merciful Father of the uni-
> verse. . . .
> (Under the influence of this new impulse, and scrupulously
> believing in the wisdom and necessity of the change,) Mark

Heathcote announced to the community, in which he had now
sojourned more than twenty years, that he intended for a second time to establish his altars in the wilderness. $(15)^2$

Mark Heathcote's decision to uproot his family and make "his
second pilgrimage . . . into scenes of renewed bodily suffering,
privation, and danger" follow the same logic as did his original
move from England (Davis 8, 7). As Cotton Mather had to
admit in the *Magnalia,* "some unhappy contests . . . grew into
an alienation that could not be cured without such a parting,
and yet, indeed, hardly so kind a parting, as that whereto once
Abraham and Lot were driven" (83). While acknowledging, as
we shall later see, the remarkable leadership Heathcote provides
his own community, so that he, like Governor Bellingham and
the other elders of Hawthorne's Boston, "stood up for the welfare of the state like a line of cliffs against a tempestuous tide,"
Cooper sees a core of radicalness at the center of Heathcote's
being (169). Where Hawthorne shows us the Puritan strength
and stuff of founders in Hester's radical heart, Cooper shows
us the stuff of radical rebels in his Puritan founder.

This sense that a germ of society's dissolution is inherent in
the act of founding permeates Cooper's thinking about politics.
It does so, I think, because of a remarkable fit between Cooper's
conscious assessment of the political scene and an unconscious
sensitivity to the fragility of order. By linking the metaphors
of revolution and frontier, Cooper forecasts that as long as there
is a frontier the Republic will remain in a state of uneasy equilibrium, on the verge either of advancing toward its great potential for good or retreating toward social disorder. More
frightening still, the rich resources of America would insure that
the new disorder would not be primitive, but would proceed
from moral and political decadence. Cooper fears a social and
political Frankenstein – a country driven forward by a powerful
economy after its heart and conscience are dead. Those readers
who still find themselves compelled by Cooper's work usually
credit his sense of history and the remarkably beautiful passages
in his prose cited by critics like Winters and Dekker. But perhaps
most of all, it is Cooper's sense of living always on the brink
of violence and darkness that appeals to readers who feel threatened with extinction.

In novels like *The Prairie* or *The Chainbearer,* the desire to escape social authority is a more explicit motive of the pioneer. Cooper expressed more broadly his fear that leaving the father's house would release man's baser nature. For Cooper, human nature was a constant in civilization or in the wilderness. But in civilization, laws and manners channeled selfishness toward constructive work that would advance the fortunes of individuals and communities. Men like Judge Temple, the Littlepages, and even Natty Bumppo are not selfless; they are men with powerful egos harnessed by values Cooper asks us selectively to approve. But without manners, without laws, without codes that have developed to protect the shared interests of community or tribe, these powerful egos become destructive.

Cooper's anxieties are most fully expressed in *The Chainbearer,* a study devoted entirely to the negative potential of the Abrahamic paradigm. Cooper casts Aaron Timberman as a degenerate descendant of the Puritans; his family's library consists of three books – "a fragment of a Bible, Pilgrim's Progress, and an almanac that was four years old" (268). He gives his sons the names of "the prophets and law givers of old" – Tobit, Nathaniel, Moses, Daniel, Zephania – and drives his tribe of twelve into the wilderness as if he were a nomad in Canaan (241). The impulse that prompted Heathcote to move his family twice becomes the guiding principle of the later New Englander's life. Thousandacres and his wife pick up their stakes seventeen times on their westward exodus from society and so personify the assumption that movement rather than stability will lead to success – one of the frontier's most enduring legacies to American society. Aaron Timberman claims for himself the stature of an Abraham or Moses, but he recognizes no authority higher than himself. As his name suggests, he is a false patriarch: not a Moses, but an Aaron bringing destruction on his people by leading them to worship a molten calf of gold. His plans to found a community in the wilderness end in disorder and brutality.

To Cooper, the patriarch's willingness to desert the firesides of his forefathers explained not only the westward migration but also its destructive rapidity. Although Heathcote uses communal worship as a way of exercising his authority over his family, he conceives of worship primarily as an intimate dialogue between God and the individual. Such rites are bound to no particular altar or place. When King Philip confronts Heathcote late in the novel and asks him why the white men left the land God gave them across the ocean, Heathcote reveals the theological assumption behind the migration:

> "Wretched and blind worshipper of Apollyon!" interrupted the Puritan, "we are not of the idolatrous and foolish-minded! It hath been accorded to us to know the Lord; to his chosen worshippers, all regions are alike." (372)

The last words reverberate through all of Cooper's frontier fiction. The Puritans' religion destroys their sense of place.

Although the initial success of Heathcote's experiment depends on his ability to yoke natural cycles to the service of his people and to create a garden out of the wilderness, Heathcote disavows the budding affection between man and his surroundings. It is an earthly vanity to be suppressed. Inheriting secularized versions of that attitude, later generations of pioneers like Billy Kirby, Ishmael Bush, and Aaron Timberman repeatedly invade the wilderness, cutting down trees with nearly ritual regularity in Cooper's fiction. As Tocqueville noted, such men "early broke the ties that bound them to their natal earth" (I, 295). Heathcote's declaration that "all regions are alike" leads to the endemic disrespect for nature blighting the sacred groves.

The lost sense of *patria* had, in Cooper's vision of American history, even more serious consequences. The New England legacy that encouraged continual movement bore responsibility for the tragic genocidal war; it brought European and Native American cultures into conflict at a speed that precluded the slow adaptation of one race to the other. With its double plot – the first half describing the settling of the valley, the second half concerned with the captivity of the patriarch's granddaughter and the issue of her marriage to an Indian warrior – the book's very structure argues that the settlement of America and the problem of race are inseparable. Convinced that their fate is directed by God, the Heathcotes are unable to see the moral problems of their move to the frontier (Davis xiv). The patriarch believes he is fleeing temptation, only to fall into an unrecognized sin that he shares with his race. The second-generation leaders complacently accept a degenerate heavenly "design" that assumes the superiority of the white race and justifies the extermination of the red.

According to Cooper's paradigm, Heathcote's errand in the wilderness asserts that his salvation takes precedence over being a good son, loyal to the traditions of his forefathers. That assertion elicits with anxious immediacy a corollary question. Could the rebel against his own father be a good father himself, or would his egotism, having prevailed over filial duty, undermine paternal feeling as well? To the historical novelist, who had absorbed the familial metaphor as the primary expression of America's relationship to Europe and the past, this second question became central to any examination of the nation's future. Would America's revolutionary origins prevent the establishment of a political system committed to preserve and protect future generations of sons and daughters? Would each migration to the frontier, reenacting, as Cooper held, a quasi-revolutionary assertion of self over community, disrupt beneficial continuities between past and future and leave America always vulnerable to the selfish political will of the moment? Would the pursuit of freedom by the powerful inevitably restrict the freedom of the weak? In *The Wept,* Cooper used the paradigmatic story of Abraham's willingness to sacrifice Isaac to answer that a man willing to renounce his forefathers might well sacrifice the future of his family.

The first half of *The Wept,* documenting Heathcote's leadership of the community, ends by reenacting a second critical moment in Abraham's life. After Abraham left his father's house for the wilderness, the Lord commanded him a second time: "Take now thy son, thine only son Isaac, whom thou lovest, and get thee into the land of Moriah; and offer him there for a burnt offering upon one of the mountains which I will tell thee of" (Gen. 22:2). Standing over the ashes of his community, Heathcote struggles to comprehend within his religious vision the death of its defenders and the loss of his granddaughter to Indian captivity. (In a moment, I'll return to the substitution of female offspring for male.) The Puritan voices his readiness to lay "like Abraham of old, the infant of his love, a willing offering at thy feet" (240). Though the Biblical precedent endows his exodus with grandeur, the scene's true power originates in the high tension between Heathcote's reading of the settlement's ordained destruction and Cooper's directive to take note of the human cost exacted by the patriarch's vision.

In calling up the image of Abraham as a rebel, Cooper's patriarch follows Thomas Hooker, the actual founder of Hartford, in placing the purity of his religious mission above the affectionate ties of family and community. Pointing to the sacrifice of Isaac, Hooker said, "This is that which God requireth not only of *Abraham* but of all beleevers [sic]: *Whosoever will be my Disciple,* saith Christ, *must forsake father, and mother, and wife, and children, and houses, and lands: yea, and he must deny himselfe, and take up his Crosse, and follow me*" (Morgan 177). The historical precedent puts Heathcote's moral seriousness beyond reproof; that the communal disaster leaves his faith and sense of purpose unshaken commands our admiration and, as McWilliams notes, confirms Heathcote's right to rule as patriarch (253). But Cooper's nineteenth-century sensibility ironically intrudes. Heathcote too readily devotes his son's offspring to the wilderness; he goes too far in asking his community to accept *their* tribulation as part of God's judgment on *his* soul (Franklin 136).

Without denying his right to speak for the community, Cooper emphasizes the egocentricity of his exhortation:

> He that hath given freely, hath taken away; and one, that hath long smiled upon my weakness, hath now veiled his face in anger. I have known him in his power to bless; it was meet that I should see him in his displeasure. A heart that was waxing confident would have hardened in its pride. (235)

His prayer is "interrupted by a heavy groan, that [bursts] from the chest" of the child's father (240). The patriarch's egotism seems less grotesque than, for example, Orgon's claim in *Tartuffe* – "My mother, children, brother, and wife could die, / And I'd not feel a single moment's pain" – but Cooper's irony only mutes Molière's exaggerated expression of Puritan zeal (1.5). Both writers recognize that religious inspiration, when opposed to social tradition, can release voracious egocentricity from necessary restraint.

Cooper's perspective suggests that Heathcote's responsibility for his granddaughter's fate does not turn, as he claims, on his excessive pride in the things of this world, but rather on the spiritual pride that directed his children to the wilderness. The rhetoric of Heathcote's allusion to Abraham's filial offering echoes his earlier farewell address to the elders of Massachusetts Bay Colony:

> Much have I endured, as you know, in *quitting the earthly mansion of my fathers,* and in encountering the dangers of the sea and land for the faith; and, rather than let go its hold, will I once more cheerfully devote to the howling wilderness, ease, *offspring,* and, should it be the will of Providence, life itself!
> (16; emphasis added)

In this almost typological way, Cooper links the injuries suffered by Heathcote's family to the patriarch's earlier break with society.

To Cooper, the example of Abraham illustrates the problematic psychology of rebellion. By breaking with society to free himself from repugnant authority, the rebel succeeded, whether consciously or not, in achieving for himself an authority over his family and immediate community equal to or greater than the original authority he found intolerable. Among the radical and separatist extremes of American Protestantism, Philip Greven has found a consistent "evangelical" family pattern. Like Heathcote, the evangelical father often moved his family away from the more moderate Puritan community that he felt had compromised its faith (25). By keeping the family isolated from, and suspicious of, alternative social and religious authority, he claimed unmitigated and unappealable authority over his children.

That Abraham's example could support this pattern of rebellion and assertion is evident even in the case of parents of the more moderate center like John and Abigail Adams. Under the pressure of rebellion, they invoked the language of Abraham's twofold test – the willingness to give up father and son, past and future, in obedience to God. In May 1776, Abigail voiced their faith that "our country is, as it were, a secondary God, and the first and greatest parent. It is to be preferred to parents, wives, children, friends, all things" (*Letters* 168; Martin 331). To preserve liberty, Adams argued to Mercy Warren and to his wife, required passion for the public good; and then, to enforce his point, he added with fierce finality that if his children refused to follow him in this dedication, they would be dead to him (159). In the name of *liberty,* Adams asserted rigid patriarchal control over his own family. Writing only months before the formal declaration of his generation's own rebellion against England, Adams imputes his own rebelliousness to his children and then proceeds to threaten them with the punishment he risks himself. That Adams's phrasing slides somewhere between Hooker's reading of the Gospel and Orgon's fanaticism illustrates the slipperiness of radical authority.

With his own history of psychic battles against a dominant father, Cooper intuitively understood both the rebel's implicit dread of the discord released by his own break with the father and his consequent counterassertion of authority in his own right. In *The Wept,* the patriarch's threatening domination seems uppermost in Cooper's mind; in 1847 the mature novelist and comfortable paterfamilias invents a fantastic South Sea world in *The Crater* in order to give his rebellious and approved hero sufficient room to exercise, at least temporarily, his patriarchal sway. While the attitude toward the patriarch shifts across the spectrum, the pattern of rebellion followed by the reassertion of authority is a fixed part of Cooper's fictional world.

In *The Wept,* Cooper's most significant variation of the Isaac episode stands out boldly: the sacrificial victim of his Abraham is a young woman, Heathcote's missing granddaughter. In fact, each step in Heathcote's remove from society is evaluated by its cost to the women of his family. Cooper specifies that "the very day [Heathcote] landed in the long-wished-for asylum, his wife made him the father of a noble boy, a gift that she bestowed at the melancholy price of her own existence" (13–14). In order to establish Heathcote's male line in America, a woman dies and the natural order of generations is upset; Heathcote's expectation to "pay the debt of nature" before his much younger wife is contradicted (14). The young and female are sacrificed to the plans of the old and male – a pattern repeated in the next two generations by the captivity of Heathcote's granddaughter, her early death, and the death of her grieving mother.

In this Cooper anticipates Hawthorne's account of Puritan repression in *The Scarlet Letter*; Hester's marginal state and Pearl's reverse migration to Europe signal the exclusion of directly expressed sensuality and cultural richness under the demands of the New England frontier. Although Cooper's metaphor is less complexly suggestive, the extermination of the female line signals the loss on the frontier both of moral refinement and of a natural affectionate check on racial and moral absolutism. The granddaughter's death, after she has married and borne a son to her Indian captor, wipes out even the distant possibility of reconciliation between Indians and immigrants.

To fix the pattern of male accomplishments built on female sacrifices, Cooper approaches outright sarcasm in explaining how Heathcote names his first-born American boy Content. Once again calling attention to the patriarch's break with ancestral tradition, Cooper notes that instead of naming the child Mark, the "baptismal appellation . . . of most of his ancestors, for two or three centuries," Heathcote hopes, "by a sort of delusive piety," to furnish "a commendable evidence of his own desperate resignation to the will of Providence, in causing him to be publicly christened by the name of Content" (14). Each time this odd spiritual patronymic jars us, we are reminded of the child's mother swept out of the family's American history at its inception; yet, like Thomas Sutpen's first wife, another woman denied participation in a grand patriarchal design, she remains a presence throughout the romance despite her early disappearance.

The legacy of this split between male and female experience in the Puritans' migration shows up sharply not only in Cooper's later romances but also in nonfiction accounts like Tocqueville's remarkable effort to convey "a more complete notion of the trials to which the women of America. . .are often subjected" (*Democracy* II: appendix U 362).[3] Like Cooper, Tocqueville emphasized the representative status of his scene by moving into epic cadences and by closing with an uncharacteristic Biblical metaphor: "The dwelling is itself a little world, an ark of civilization amid an ocean of foliage: a hundred steps beyond it the primeval forest spreads its shades, and solitude resumes its sway" (II: 365). In form, Tocqueville's account goes on to describe the entrance of a civilized traveler into a wilderness clearing and begins with an extended account of the male pioneer, as if husbands were themselves the frontier woman's greatest trial. His "angular features and lank limbs" proclaim him, like Cooper's patriarch, a "native of New England." Behind the coolness of the frontiersman, Tocqueville discovers the "passion" of a "restless, calculating, and adventurous race of men. To conquer and civilize the backwoods," to exert his control over the wilderness, he "puts trees to death," mutilating them with his axe. By contrast, his wife, though of an "appearance superior to her condition," has a cast of deep "religious resignation"; "her delicate limbs appear shrunken; her features are drawn in, her eye is wild and melancholy" (II: 362 – 64).

The fatal suffering of the Heathcote women is an archetypal expression of the split between male and female conceptions of the frontier – a split documented in the entire tradition of frontier literature. The male pioneer might boast of making the earth bear fruit, but this mythical union of masculine and feminine was often accompanied by an exploitative relationship between real men and real women.

Paradoxically, Cooper conjoins his attack on the patriarch's egotism with his admiration for Heathcote's assertion of patriarchal authority. Even Cooper's carefully handled irony would fail to weld together such divergent attitudes were they not related at deeper psychological and intellectual levels. Cooper, like Melville, had his reasons for wanting to identify with patriarchal authority even as he constantly chafed at it. Though Cooper's irony keeps the two attitudes simultaneously before the reader, the differing responses are in a sense sequential. If, as a quasi-revolutionary act, Heathcote's migration to the frontier releases man's egotism from the controls represented by the father's house, it creates on the frontier a vulnerable society calling for strong patriarchal authority, which Heathcote in all his egotism can provide. While Cooper attacks Heathcote for his rebellion, he finds in the very sources of that rebellion – in the patriarch's will and self-command – the authority needed to minimize, or even redeem, the cost of his break with the past.

That periods of political retrenchment follow periods of revolution is a truism of nineteenth-century European politics and of the history of our own Constitution. In *Home as Found*, Eric Sundquist describes Cooper's longing for patriarchal order in Freudian terms: Cooper's attack on small-town American democracy in the 1830s represents "that stage in the community's development at which the exhilaration of democratic equality will give way to a ritual veneration of the founding fathers of the country, whether Washington and Judge Cooper or Natty Bumppo" (16); Greven describes the post-Revolutionary retreat from radicalism as a reaction to the Revolution's failed evangelical promise – that it would eradicate decadent tendencies in colonial society (Greven 354; Heimert 481). But as clarifying as these models can be, Cooper's sense of irony and paradox improves on them by revealing that models with clear stages often make distinct what is in reality mixed. As John Adams's letters suggest, the desire to associate with the father's authority reveals itself at the very moment of the decision to rebel. The apparent contradiction between Cooper's attack on Heathcote and his admiration of patriarchal authority does not split apart *The Wept* because Cooper succeeds in demonstrating that the advantages and liabilities of patriarchal power are thoroughly intertwined.

The familial relationship between community and leader remained Cooper's primary model of good government. At its best, it represented an unforced hierarchy based on the citizen's respect rather than on the imposition of the leader's will. Reading *The Wept*, one senses that Cooper's strong attraction to the clear hierarchy of the Puritan community allows him to overcome his general distrust of latter-day New Englanders. In its insistence that people were equal before God, but not to each other, Puritan theology supported Cooper's faith that the "great equality of condition" in the early stages of society would allow a natural hierarchy to emerge. As if by God's design, the physical hardships of the American wilderness stripped away unjust inequality and elevated naturally superior talents to prominence. In terms of age, intellect, skill, economics, and birth, men and

women fell into patterns of God-created superiority and inferiority – patterns that structured the interlocking orders of family, church, and state (Morgan 18). In Cooper's setting forth of
an organic hierarchy, as in the Puritan original, a passive idiom
tries to screen out the conflict inherent in the erection of any
social order. Though he may not have wished it so, Cooper
recorded the more likely consequence of relative equality in *The
Pioneers* and in later tales: fierce competition for prominence.
However, even when he comments ironically on the substance
of Heathcote's patriarchal pronouncements, in *The Wept* Cooper
has unreserved admiration for his ability to hold the community
together: "They listened, therefore, with respect, nor did an
impious smile, or an impatient glance, escape the lightest-
minded of their number during his exhortations, though the
homilies of the old man were neither very brief, nor particularly
original" (24).

Cooper's natural and architectural settings nearly always reflect his concern for organic social hierarchy. The "natural distinctions" that "choice and inclination drew . . . in the ordinary
intercourse of the inmates of the Heathcote family" print themselves on the design of their dwelling; young men and women
of the community, though not of the Heathcotes' immediate
family, work at household industries by the enormous kitchen
fire; but "A door communicated with an inner and superior
apartment" where "the principal personages of the family were
seated" among "armorial bearings" and "a few other articles,
of a fashion so antique, and of ornaments so ingenious and rich,
as to announce that they had been transported from beyond the
sea" (37 – 38).

In his admiration for the cohesive hierarchy of patriarchal
government, Cooper placed more emphasis on the responsibilities of the leader than on the obligations of the led. He celebrated Heathcote's leadership because the Puritan assumed and
fulfilled total responsibility for the citizens of his settlement.
His ironic skepticism toward Heathcote's egotism competes with
a balancing fear of impotent authority. When he assessed the
failure of presidential leadership in *The American Democrat*, he
found that "the history of the country shows ten instances of
presidents evading responsibility, to one of their abusing power"

(35). Although Heathcote had endangered his family by imposing his will and his plan of salvation on their destinies and by moving them away from the protection of society, his identification of self and community has the positive effect of making him relentlessly vigilant. Without reservation, Cooper approves Heathcote's coolness while directing his family's defense under Indian attack and the prudence of his decision to build the underground retreat that saves the family from total destruction. Content Heathcote shares his father's "equanimity" of temper under danger and voices Cooper's deepest sense of the world: "on the borders `. . . there is little security but in untiring watchfulness" (94, 96). Above all other obligations of the father, Cooper consistently placed the duty to provide physical security.

In frontier literature, from Mather's *Magnalia* to Per Hansa's fatal attempt to bring food to the snowbound settlement in *Giants in the Earth*, the rescue of a fledgling community by its founder emerges as an archetypal scene. To Mather and, I think, to other frontier writers, it represents the hope that the severe conditions of the New World will engender cohesion among the men and women clinging to its icy face. The rescue episode suppresses the more predictable results of hardship, such as dissent and uncertainty, and insists against the odds that adversity will foster a new organic unity in America to replace the cohesion of the Old World society, the established hierarchies of church and state, the traditions, celebrations, and old myths supporting social organicism. Thus, in Mather's account of John Winthrop's charity during the Puritans' first winter, the effect of his example on the community receives even more emphasis than his individual selflessness:

> . . . 'twas marvellous to see how *helpful* these good people were to one another, following the example of their most liberal governour Winthrop, who made an equal distribution of what he had in his own stores among the poor, *taking no thought for tomorrow!* (78)

In *The Pioneers*, the one unquestioned justification for Judge Temple's position of authority is his decisive action to save the settlers from discouragement and starvation during the "infancy" of the settlement. Basing the incident closely on his father's rescue of Cooperstown, Cooper inserted a footnote to claim it was "literally true!" (Beard ed. 235). But in works more fully cast as romances than the "descriptive tale" of *The Pioneers*, Cooper consistently transforms his source story of rescue from natural hardships into one more violent. In the evolving myth, more immediately fatal threats test the patriarch's vigilance.

Heathcote receives the approbation of a novelist obsessed by the consequences of paternal incompetence. In Cooper's work, the number of patriarchal figures who fail to protect their children or community is extraordinary. The pattern begins as early as *The Spy*. There Cooper treats Wharton's political neutrality as a form of moral debility threatening to the safety of his family and estate. The intervention of "Mr. Harper," Cooper's fictional representation of Washington, rescues Wharton's children from the consequences of their father's passivity. But such near misses are the exception. Paternal carelessness usually brings swift and terrible consequences. When Sergeant Dunham fails to reconnoiter his island base camp in *The Pathfinder*, Indians in ambush mortally wound him and bring down several soldiers under his charge. In *The Last of the Mohicans*, slaughter on a vaster scale descends on the troops retreating from Fort William Henry. Munro defines his paternal responsibility for the men and women of the garrison: to Major Heyward he says, "All that you see here claim alike to be my children" (250). But, dejected by defeat, Munro negotiates the terms of surrender with insufficient caution. Trusting Montcalm too easily, Munro leads the garrison out from the protection of the fort to imminent annihilation by the French Indians. The father blunders again in *Wyandotté*, when Cooper returns late in his career to the civil violence unleashed by the American Revolution. Like Heathcote, Captain Willoughby leads his family into a secluded wilderness valley where the community prospers until Indians and rebel irregulars attack it. Unlike Heathcote, however, Willoughby fails to take the most prudent course. The father's miscalculation brings instantaneous and unforgiving retribution. The Indian Wyandotté stabs Captain Willoughby from behind; marauders kill his wife and daughter after storming through the gates the father had failed to secure.

With noticeable consistency in this list of paternal failures, Indians or whites dressed as Indians bring down violent and immediate destruction on the father and his family. Taken one novel at a time, the Indian ambush seems merely a formulaic requirement of the adventure story, but taken over an entire career, the ambush emerges as representative of a more essential insecurity hovering ubiquitously over Cooper's characters. Although readers may well share Mark Twain's impatience at the repetitiveness of such incidents, they illustrate Cooper's acute sense of society's fragile hold over man's innate savageness. That a father's mistake so often exposes this vulnerability not only points to the psychological origins of the violence in Cooper's imaginative world, but also explains his consequent emphasis on the paternal responsibilities of leadership.

In Cooper's fiction, death comes to the paternal figure when he least expects it, just as it did to his own father: the veneer of civilization cracked for a moment, and the patriarch of Cooperstown was struck down. If this was not enough to persuade the novelist of life's precariousness and the corresponding importance of security, he had sufficient brushes with mortality to teach him the lesson. His older sister was thrown from a horse and killed when Cooper was a boy. (In a late note to *The Pioneers*, Cooper refers to her as a "second mother"; although the note is formal in tone, Cooper would not have broken his habitual personal reserve unless disarmed by deep affection and bereavement for this "very near and dear" sibling and perhaps even by a sense of being orphaned that had been renewed by re-reading his earlier novel.) Two of his own children died before reaching the age of ten; his brother Isaac was killed in a wrestling match with his brother-in-law; and his other three brothers all died prematurely between 1813 and 1819. At thirty Cooper was left as the head of a large family and was responsible not only for the welfare of his sisters-in-law and their children but also for the remnants of his father's estate and the debts of his brothers. Although a shrewd and farsighted man, William Cooper had not planned well enough to protect his family against all the contingencies that befell them.

While the son obviously understood that his father had died the victim of a crime, he may well have felt resentment at the series of events that placed him in a position of extraordinary responsibility and deprived him of the legacy he had expected. His freedom had been compromised. Whether or not Cooper consciously blamed his father's expansive, rough-edged nature, the father who had been a victim in life became the careless father in his fiction. The incompetence of Willoughby, Monro, Dunham, and Wharton is commensurate not with William Cooper's actual irresponsibility but with James Fenimore Cooper's own sense of life's insecurity and the responsibilities he had acquired as the patriarch of his own large family.

This background underscores Mark Heathcote's achievement. His caution and foresight establish him as an ideal leader: his preparation of the underground refuge acquires metaphoric significance. The Heathcote household retreats into a fortification built like a Chinese box – a tunnel within a well shaft, within a blockhouse, within a palisade – and its structure, like the crevice and burrow of Frost's drumlin woodchuck, comes to stand for the extraordinary prudence required in a threatening world; the slightest lapse of vigilance courts disaster. By way of contrast, in the second section of the romance only the nearly miraculous intervention of Conanchet saves the settlers from the consequences of the inadequate precautions taken by the second-generation leaders of Wish-Ton-Wish.

If the patriarch's first great virtue is his vigilant response to the outside world, his second is his active ability to transform that world. Through his familial government, Heathcote extends his sense of rigorous personal morality into the public sphere. This elevation of public morality, like his vigilance, is a positive corollary of the patriarch's egotistical identification of the community's fate with his own. As Hawthorne also recognized, the Puritans' plans to take away Hester's parental responsibility for Pearl and their ability to stand up "for the welfare of the state like a line of cliffs against a tempestuous tide" flow from similar patriarchal impulses. The iron Endicott of the Red Cross and Winthrop, whose followers read the dusky portent marking his death as A for Angel, are Janus faces of the American Abraham.

Behind Cooper's respect for Heathcote's influence on public morality lie two assumptions: not only that the example of one man can elevate the state, but that the private morality of the best men rises above national codes. During the first stages of settlement, when the natural leader has the opportunity to exert his personal authority, his superiority will extend throughout the body of his community. In Cooper, as in Hawthorne, Cather, and Faulkner, the decline in stature of later generations all the more emphatically elicits admiration for the stern character of the founders. Contemplating the incompetence, pettiness, lassitude, and ignorance of the second generation, Cooper suspends his judgmental tone toward Heathcote, just as Hawthorne's appreciation of the New England patriarchs, even of Endicott, increases when he considers the reductive frivolity of Morton or the relics of his own era ensconced in the Custom House.

The superiority of the founders' values, articulated by Content Heathcote during the second half of *The Wept,* emerges in contrast to the colonial government's vicious attitude toward the New England Indians. Heathcote's conviction that his personal destiny is guided by God may lead him to misunderstand his obligations to forefathers and family, but it also causes him to be just and moderate in his dealing with the Indians. When they destroy his settlement, Heathcote interprets the raid as God's chastisement against his pride, and, on that basis, he cautions the young men he sends for help against revenge:

> I ask not vengeance on the deluded and heathenish imitators of the worshippers of Moloch. They have ignorantly done this evil. Let no man arm in behalf of wrongs of one sinful and erring. Rather let them look into the secret abominations of their own hearts, in order that they crush the living worm, which, by gnawing on the seeds of a healthful hope, may yet destroy the fruits of the promise in their own souls. . . . Depart, and bear in mind, that ye are messengers of peace. (233)

In *Political Justice in a Republic,* John McWilliams notes that "because there is no civil law on the frontier, Cooper's borderers must turn their definitions of the moral law into civil action" (242). When the moral standards of the patriarch are as exacting as Heathcote's, this transformation of personal vision into public policy elevates civil morality to its highest level. Heathcote relates history to the state of his soul, and, therefore, his humility before God tempers his public acts.

To weigh the colony's policy against Heathcote's moderation, Cooper exactly parallels the patriarch's warning in a later scene introduced by an epigraph from *The Winter's Tale:* "Be certain what you do sir; lest your justice / Prove violence" (300). A messenger from the Connecticut Council comes to Wish-Ton-Wish, reports on King Philip's raids along the Massachusetts frontier, and tries to enlist troops for a retaliatory expedition. When Content Heathcote expresses doubts about the morality of the council's campaign, the messenger is staggered. He can't comprehend the younger Heathcote's effort to subdue the idea of revenge for the loss of his daughter by consciousness of his own sin. Cooper captures the bureaucrat's uneasiness:

> "This is well, Captain Heathcote, and in exceeding conformity with the most received doctrines, . . . but it hath little connexion with present duties. My charge beareth especial concern with the further destruction of the Indians, rather than to any inward searchings into the condition of our own mental misgivings." (305)

Belittling Content's moral objections by referring to them as mere "mental misgivings," the government representative refuses to set warfare against the Indians in a moral context. On the contrary, he uses Biblical rhetoric to place the Indian outside the national and racial group to which he'll selectively apply his morality: when it is "a matter of dominion and possession of these fair lands, that the Lord hath given – why, sir," the messenger continues, "then I say that, like the Israelites dealing with the sinful occupants of Canaan, it behoveth us to be true to each other, and to look upon the heathen with a distrustful eye" (306). His rhetoric cloaks the transformation of justifiable defense into planned genocide.

Having lost the sense of personal morality characteristic of the patriarch's familial government, the colony rationalizes immoral policies in terms of public necessity and soon participates in the very acts of slaughter they decry. Content Heathcote listens sadly as the nameless colonial agent coolly announces a bounty for scalps at the end of the pious exhortations of the council. The government suggests that soldiers prepare themselves by deep self-examination, that congregations deal severely with backsliders, who may provoke God's wrath, that villages call up their militia, "and fourthly, it is contemplated to counteract the seeds of vengeance, by setting a labor-earning price on the heads of our enemies" (308). Cooper has a fine ear for the passive syntax ("it has been contemplated") and the New Englanders' financial rationale ("a labor-earning price") used to obfuscate the council's moral responsibility. In fact, they propose that scalping for money saves the scalpers from the sin of vengeance. Content Heathcote objects to the bounty, but by this second stage of frontier development he has insufficient influence to affect the community's policy. As Cooper argues in a later work, "Individuals, *may* be, and sometimes *are,* reasonably upright – but, *bodies* of men, I much fear, never. The latter escape responsibility by dividing it" (*Wyandotté* 228–29).

Among the second-generation leaders, the negative tendencies of the patriarch's rebellion come to dominate in a particularly dangerous way – not by rejecting outright the morality of the patriarch, but rather by perverting it. They speak in Heathcote's idiom, but it has become merely a disguise for their self-serving egotism. The trial of the Indian to whom the village leaders owe their survival is a travesty of patriarchal judgment: "The question was gravely considered, and it was decided with a deep and conscientious sense of the responsibility of those who acted as judges. Several hours were passed in deliberation, Meek [Wolfe, the second-generation divine,] opening and closing the deliberations by solemn prayers" (452). In fact, their decision is an act of moral cowardice. Out of fear of their Indian allies, the commissioners of the colony turn their captive over to the revenge of his Pequot and Mohegan captors. They know their own duplicity, but rationalize "the aspect of timeserving" by perverting the key terms of Heathcote's faith (452). They disguise an "act of positive cruelty" as God's judgment: "The triumph of thy evil nature hath been short, and now cometh the judgment!" (454, 451). In a flurry of spectacular double talk, they invoke Providence, mercy, humility, necessity, and even submission:

> "Mercy is a quality of heavenly origin," replied Meek Wolfe, "and it should not be perverted to defeat the purposes of heavenly wisdom. Azazel must not triumph, though the tribe of the Narragansetts should be swept with the besom of de-

> struction. Truly we are an erring and a fallible race, Captain
> Heathcote; and the greater, therefore, the necessity that we
> submit, without rebellion, to the inward monitors that are
> implanted, by grace, to teach us the road to our duty – "
>   "I cannot consent to shed blood, now that strife hath
> ceased," hastily interrupted Content. (422)

Having initially hoped to exercise "an ulterior discretion in the
case," Content Heathcote must now acknowledge that the hope
of final control over an inferior second generation is delusory
(428). As Cooper witnesses their unchecked strength, his prose
cracks into open scorn.

From *The Pioneers* to *The Crater,* the patriarchal era is brief.
As communities expand, the familial relationship between the
leader and his people grows weaker. Cooper associates the momentary organic cohesion of patriarchy with his own childhood
at Cooperstown and, more important, with the "infancy" of
civilization repeatedly re-created on the frontier. Although the
westward migration exposes the community to the moral and
physical dangers of breaking from society, it also offers the possibility of a return to a familial sense of security and order. This,
and not the romantic appeal of the wilderness, is Cooper's primary reason for returning so often to the frontier settlement in
his later novels.

Through Cooper's admiration for the patriarch runs a deep
current of longing for public recognition of his own authority.
In a scene that seems wonderfully revealing of the unvoiced
ambitions of a writer, Heathcote, leaving his community by
sea, as Cooper left America in 1826, sees before him the entire
community lining his path in silent respect. That Cooper aspired
to publicly recognized authority like Heathcote's or Governor
Bellingham's is evident in his earliest plans to write romances
for each of the thirteen original colonies, in the nonfiction works
of his middle career, and in the running political jeremiad that
often overwhelms the novels of the late 1830s and 1840s.

Identification with the patriarch lifted a sentence to which his
own theory of history condemned him. As the son of a wilderness founder, Cooper was himself a member of the second
generation, whose decline he not only lamented but declared
nearly inevitable. He concurred with Tocqueville's estimation

that "American statesmen of the present day are very inferior
to those who stood at the head of affairs fifty years ago. This
is as much a consequence of circumstances as of the laws of the
country" (I, 203). When Cooper grossly inflated the seriousness
of the antirent movement along the Hudson, his attempt to create circumstances worthy of the founders' original heroism became painfully evident. By insisting on his status as founder –
an exception, like Content Heathcote, to the general decline –
he struggled against the crippling sense of inferiority suffered,
as George Forgie argues, by his generation. He refused Charles
Francis Adams's stoic acceptance of a lesser fate: "It is for us to
preserve and not to create" (157). Cooper knew from the inside
out his paradigmatic story of a rebel who claims exclusive patriarchal authority over the next generation. As a writer, he
transformed historical "preservation" into an art of original creation that endowed him with authority. He claimed for himself
the American promise, as Crèvecoeur had defined it, to be a
self-created man able to create his own patrimony – to be both
rebel and founder.

2

Family Origins and Patriarchal Designs

In the spring of 1820, with no apparent warning, James Cooper decided to become a writer. His creative life, like Whitman's, came to a boil. So radical was the transmutation that it is more difficult to recognize the latent novelist in the gentleman farmer than to divine *Leaves of Grass* in the pages of *The Democratic Review* or the Brooklyn *Eagle*. Yet in order to understand why Cooper persistently identified with the social authority wielded by frontier patriarchs, it is essential to know the pressures responsible for the alchemic change of his thirty-first year.

The mythology of Cooper's transformation follows a formulaic pattern. Impatient with reading aloud a tedious, imported novel of manners, Cooper reportedly threw it down and declared to his wife that he could write a better one. Not unaccustomed to her husband's flamboyant self-assertion after nine years of marriage, Susan De Lancey Cooper challenged him to prove it. In her daughter's words: "Our Mother laughed at the idea, as the height of absurdity – he who disliked writing even a letter, that he should write a book!!"[1] After setting aside an initial moral tale, he sequestered himself in the drawing room each morning until he produced *Precaution* (Beard 24).

At no point is it more important to embrace D. H. Lawrence's caveat "Never trust the artist. Trust the tale" than when approaching stories about the origin of a writer's career. In retrospect, years of struggle may acquire a glamorous patina, but surely it is more appealing to imagine oneself a Dr. Johnson, a Coleridge, a Rilke, a Faulkner suddenly spinning off a tour de force in a few late night hours or weeks. In such legends, there lies not merely justification of our plodding past but hope for our transformation tomorrow, perhaps even tonight. Yet the problematic nature of Cooper's story stems less from its possible inaccuracy than from its apparent inadequacy. As James F. Beard implies, the legend that Cooper began writing "accidentally" cannot explain either why Cooper rose to a challenge doubtless aimed at countless other complainers or why his response became a life-long career (xxi). Taken at face value, the story's gentility casts the beginning of Cooper's career in an inappropriately casual light and contributes to the persistent, reductive assessment of Cooper as a somehow preliterary artist. However, taken as a carefully filtered symptom of Cooper's angry dissatisfaction with himself, the tale has a good deal to tell about a need to write so compelling that it launched the most prolific career in American letters before those of James and Howells.

The element of challenge in the legendary story gains particular significance by its duplication at two further breakthrough moments in Cooper's early career. Both *The Last of the Mohicans* and *The Pilot* were written in response to challenges similar in their apparent casualness. In 1826, *The Last of the Mohicans* sealed Cooper's quick ascension to literary prominence in America and Europe and elevated Natty Bumppo to the rank of paradigmatic American hero. On a tour to the caves under Glens Falls, Cooper's English visitor, Lord Stanley, urged him to develop the scene's romantic possibilities in fiction. Under Cooper's shaping, the benign challenge became an invitation to leave the wilderness of his childhood, reanimated in *The Pioneers* (1823), and enter the darker tracings of American history and of his imagination. With *The Pilot* (1823), Cooper not only opened an entire side of his career, eventually resulting in nearly a dozen naval romances and *The History of the Navy of the United States of America* (1839), but also fathered the sea tale and its Leviathan progenitors Melville and Conrad (Philbrick). After successes with *The Spy* (1821) and *The Pioneers,* Cooper lowered his guard, and his openness about *The Pilot*'s generative spark allows us to see further into his original self-transformation.

In more precise terms, the origins of *The Pilot* repeat and define the elements of his wife's earlier challenge.[2] During a gathering of his friends in the winter of 1823, conversation turned to Scott and his recent romance *The Pirate* (1821). Cooper, an ex-naval officer, bridled at the group's admiration for a story riddled with nautical inaccuracies. He vowed to write a true romance of the sea that would put the master romancer in his proper place. His companions greeted his vaunt with disbelief and questioned whether the reading public would be able to follow the intricacies of naval hardware and etiquette, or have any interest in doing so. Any doubts they may have had about his abilities were kept to themselves. On his return home from the meeting, Cooper outlined the plot of *The Pilot* (SC 52–53).[3]

That Cooper's art emerged from a challenge suggests how closely Cooper's motives for writing were bound to his own sense of self-worth and to his deep concern with other people's estimation of him. While some writers work from a particular observed event, or a memory recollected in tranquillity, Cooper returned to his experience as a naval officer under competitive pressure. He responded to the question implicit in all challenges: did he have the ability to fulfill his promise. A second, equally important element informed the pattern: Cooper himself engineered the challenge by making an extravagant claim. To his wife, the man on record as a nonwriter boasted that he could pen a better book; to his friends, that he could not only surpass but even shame the most popular writer of fiction in the world. He compelled his own performance, throwing up his own hoops before jumping through them. To take the pattern as a whole: a seemingly extravagant claim produced a challenge that, in turn, provoked an artistic response commensurate with the original claim of self-worth.

As one might suspect, however, the pattern played out in public implies an interior debate antecedent to the articulated boast. The extravagant claim and the doubting challenge repeat Cooper's divided estimation of himself; they display the severe disparity between his expectations and his self-deprecating assessment. Though he had reason to feel more confident by the time he conceived *The Pilot,* habit and multiplying financial entanglements called him back to the pattern of boast, challenge, and response – a pattern etched on his psyche during the decade preceding his decision to become a writer, when the guise of genteel accomplishment gave way under the pressure of increasing self-doubt.

On most occasions, the assertion that one can write a better novel, give a better speech, or run a safer subway with one's hands tied is a delusory way of asserting self-importance in the face of contrary evidence. The boast harmlessly substitutes for actual exertion. But in Cooper's case, the contending impulses expressed in his boast overpowered inertia by a kind of egocentric logic. For Cooper, living without great distinction was intolerable. Since, in his own severe self-judgment, he had not yet distinguished himself, Cooper felt an unusually deep sense of isolation. No one recognized his true merit. His profound loneliness produced in turn a greater need to break through and command acknowledgment. He must make himself known through writing.[4]

In the course of Natty Bumppo's career, Cooper made a virtue of solitude, but his first account of an isolato smarts with the thinly disguised pain of a misunderstood life.[5] Cooper wrote *The Spy* in the first flush of his self-transformation into a writer. Completing *Precaution,* Cooper poured himself into *The Spy* without pause. In two weeks, he surged through the first sixty pages of manuscript and the telling outline of Harvey Birch's situation. In hidden service to his country, Harvey Birch travels the roads of Cooper's own Westchester County. At best, people see him as a shiftless peddler cynically pursuing his own interest while others sacrifice life and livelihood; at worst, they revile and persecute him as a traitor. Though he feels strong filial affection for his aged father and takes unstinting paternal interest in the young hero and heroine, he does so in secret – his virtues as son and father are hidden from the public eye. Even Mr. Harper, the disguised Washington, underestimates him, meeting his unflagging service with an offer of money and the skepticism habitually accorded to mercenaries. But for the spy, money in itself means nothing. Harvey is a man unknown, without a father or a home, a man whose sense of self receives no confirmation from the society around him. For such a man, Cooper well knew, there is only one sufficient reward. Finally comprehending Harvey's uncorrupted patriotism, Washington at last answers his hopes by acknowledging his secret self: "Now, indeed, I know you" (539).

It may seem paradoxical that a man as apparently sociable and active as James Cooper could have felt unknown and unrecognized. During the first decade of his marriage, Cooper founded and actively participated in the agricultural and religious societies of his community. He took an interest in politics, joined the militia, and took part in neighborhood theatricals. In addition to many shorter migrations and briefer domiciles, he twice established his growing family on new estates, building a house on each occasion, clearing trees, setting out pastures and fields. Yet for Cooper, these activities did not add up. They might suffice as the peripheral distinctions of true accomplishment, but they did not constitute the accomplishment itself. In this inability to credit his own worth, Cooper ran abruptly into his father's career.

James Cooper's most obvious problem was the sheer magnitude of his father's achievement. It not only provided the measure of authority the son would have to attain, but set the very terms in which he would think and write of authority for the rest of his life. Having begun life as a wheelwright's apprentice, William Cooper became the friend of powerful men in a powerful state at a critical period of national political development (Dekker 1–8). In the year of James's birth, William Cooper moved his family to the wilderness. Extending his authority beyond his family of five sons and two daughters, the patriarch guided the larger migration of his settlers for over thirty years. An intensely physical man, he insisted on playing a frank, personal, and commanding role in their lives. Furthermore, William Cooper knew that his position on the frontier was representative – that his work, however large as an independent accomplishment, had even more significance because it enacted, in the largest possible terms, the process of building a nation repeated on the frontier, north and south, east and west (Franklin 9).

In the process of growing up, most children must readjust their original view of the world as centered on their parents. As they see beyond the circumference of the family, they learn, sometimes painfully, that other people assign less importance to their parents and may even look down on them. The reassessment raises questions about the father and mother's ability to protect the child, and since the father serves as the son's most immediate definition of manhood, the diminishment of the father may trigger the son's first confrontation with the reduced part he himself will play when he moves beyond his childhood circle. On the other hand, the gradual diminishment of the father has an important liberating effect, in that it enables the son to believe that the world will afford room for another adult male.

William Cooper's position on the New York frontier inevitably retarded the natural diminishment of his presence. When James Cooper looked beyond his family to the community, he saw his father still at the center of a patronymically named village; when he looked beyond the village, he saw his father presiding as judge of the county court; even when he went to school in Albany, he had not moved beyond the limits of his father's activity or importance. The debts run up at Yale and the pranks that eventually sent him back to Cooperstown can be seen, at least in part, as an older child's efforts to test the reach of his father's command. Even when he moved decisively beyond his father's sway, as a sailor before the mast, he jumped from the pan to the fire, placing himself under the authority of a ship's captain in whom, as Melville reminds us, "lodged a dictatorship beyond which, while at sea, there was no earthly appeal" (*Benito Cereno* 9). Given this progression, it is understandable that Cooper gained leverage on his father's centrality relatively slowly. William Cooper's prominence left James with an enlarged sense of the authority he must command to win independent manhood.

In effect, Cooper's dilemma exposes the trap inherent in the patriarchal role of the founding generation. If the first generation endured the hardships of war so that the second generation could develop the arts of peace and the third practice the accomplishments of art, the intended progression up the scale of civilization was shadowed by an implicit diminution of the stature of each succeeding generation. As George Forgie and Michael Rogin noted in their histories of Lincoln and Jackson, the second generation rarely escapes the burden of its implied inferiority and,

if it succeeds, does so by strategies of accommodation and rebellion. In Cooper's case, the power of Judge Cooper to act
within his son's mind as the harsh arbiter of his worth survives
in the severe judgment James Fenimore Cooper levels at fictional
fathers throughout his thirty-year career.

Unless driven by overwhelming and focused ambition, activity meant little, or so would seem to have been the message
of William Cooper's success to his son. The more committees
and societies James Cooper joined to address particular issues,
the more he would be reminded that his father had simply assumed authority over *all* issues. William Cooper had created
not particular societies but a society in its entirety. A letter written by the senior Cooper to James's brother William catches the
unforgiving alternatives offered from parent to child – alternatives similar to the demands recorded in the Adams family
correspondence. Like John and Abigail, William Cooper expressed his fierce pride and love for his children in terms of their
relationship to the country's future. Encouragement abruptly
alternates with debilitating severity: "Here is a great country
. . . and no young man had such an opportunity as yourself of
being the first man in it. On your industry depends whether
you are to be the great good and useful man – or nothing"
(Beard xx). William Cooper's message comes through clearly:
if you want to be son to *this* father, you must measure up or
be orphaned. Although addressed to his brother, James Cooper
took the implications of his father's standards to heart: not to
be great was to be nothing.[6]

Cooper's inability to credit his early life leads once more to
the pattern of challenge informing his literary beginnings. In
the cases of *Precaution* and *The Pilot,* Cooper manipulates challenges from those people most intimate with him – his wife and
the close group of male friends so important to him in the early
1820s. In part, this maneuver guarantees the support of his "opponents"; they become his own seconds in his new enterprise.
But in their very love and affection, wife and friends also unwittingly posed a threat; they accepted him as he was. However
comforting and necessary on one level, Cooper could not rest
while people accepted the man they had witnessed in the third
decade of his life as the *real* James Cooper. What they knew and

accepted was "nothing." Friends, as well as a huge and as yet unimpressed public, must feel the pressure of his ambition. Where they saw an accomplished Westchester gentleman, Cooper saw only a blank. His preface to *Precaution* (1820) is explicit. Though he wished to be understood, he had first "to prove that the world did not know me" (Beard ed. *Pioneers* 3; Franklin 22). On a blank life, his writing would stamp a claim to authority by which others could read the true man.

The gestures of his private life reveal how thoroughly James Cooper's sense of self incorporated his father's patriarchal design. In the year of his marriage, Cooper bought a farm outside of Cooperstown where he planned to build his "seat." The details of his project are scant but significant. The land commanded a fine view of Lake Otsego, opposite the mountain outlook at The Vision, where his father had first surveyed his future empire. Cooper would follow his father and build his house out of stone, at once announcing the claim of his wealth and his desire to make a permanent impression on his country and countrymen. During its construction in 1816, he carved his wife's name and his own with the date on a foundation stone. Though nothing extraordinary, the gesture suggests the kind of self-consciousness that endows mundane events with significance. It reminds us of Keats's belief that "a Man's life of any worth is a continual allegory" (284). Carving the stone enacted his claims as a founder: against the overwhelming fact of his father's priority in Cooperstown, he asserted his right to be first on the ground. Furthermore, leaving a record in stone of his wife's name together with his own implied future progeny and served notice that he had taken over the dynastic ambitions that had propelled William Cooper's conquest of an empire large enough to divide among five sons.

By naming both farm and house "Fenimore," Cooper signaled the two primary impulses behind his plan. Once before he had tried to make the name his own; he would succeed at the height of his early career. Giving the talismanic name to his estate suggests that he then thought to invest himself totally in Cooperstown. After two years in Westchester County, where he had been unable to set up any permanent household of his own, Cooper believed his future lay on the shores of Otsego. Supported by the surrounding land, his house and family would represent his patriarchal claim. On the other hand, using his mother's surname emphatically asserts a counterimpulse to escape dependence on his father even while duplicating his patriarchal ambitions. Cooper's desire to supplant rather than succeed to his father's place persisted in sometimes quirky ways. Publishing *The Pioneers* in Paris fifteen years later, Cooper commissioned an illustration of Templeton and its environs indicative of his own patriarchal stake in Lake Otsego. Though ostensibly a guide to the narrative of first-generation settlement, the "Carte dressée pour la lecture des PIONNIERS," corrected in Cooper's own hand, omits Judge Cooper's house while anachronistically marking the location of Fenimore – "La Maison de Mr. Cooper incendrée" – even though it had burned down more than four years before and was survived by William Cooper's Mansion House (Beard ed. Plate IV).

Cooper's choice of a burial site for his infant daughter gives assurance in still more intimate terms that he accorded to the elemental moments of his own life the symbolic value he would later impress on his fictional characters. Not yet two, Elizabeth fell ill on the last day of Cooper's long-delayed exodus from his father-in-law's house and died soon after arriving at Cooperstown in the summer of 1813. Cooper's migration, like Heathcote's, exacted its cost. Cooper surprised and puzzled his family when he refused to bury his daughter in the family plot beside his father and Hannah Cooper, the older sister about whom he speaks so tenderly in *The Pioneers*. Instead, he insisted that Elizabeth be buried at the Fenimore farm on the grounds of his yet unbuilt house (SC 22). Extreme emotion exposed a basic pattern of his thinking: under the pressure of grief, land and family fuse in Cooper's mind. And it must be *his* land and family, distinct from his father's. Elizabeth would lie within the boundaries of the promised land toward which Cooper had traveled from captivity in Westchester.

Cooper's public activity during the first decade of his marriage also showed his experimentation with adopting his father's design. His founding role in both agricultural and religious societies demonstrated his sense that a Cooper's responsibilities incorporated all aspects of the community's life. To recruit new members to the Otsego Agricultural Society, he argued, as its secretary, that the society served to unite the interests of rich and poor. The example of "one neat, judicious, and economical farmer," like himself, would elevate the agricultural practice of his neighbors (37). Agriculture suited him particularly well, since it satisfied Cooper's deeply physical nature – another legacy from his father – with tentative social command. Yet the very need to institutionalize William Cooper's interest in the husbandry of his settlers forecast the increasing frustrations of this route to his father's authority.

Like the migrations of whole populations, significant movements in an individual's life depend on both push and pull. Cooper might not have needed to discover writing as his predominant strategy for gaining authority if he had not been pushed out of his first path by financial collapse and mounting family pressure. Cooper originally followed a refined version of his father's career, one more appropriate to a second-generation frontier landlord, but, nevertheless, based on his proprietorship of frontier land. As Cooper approached his thirtieth year, however, the ancestral ground at Cooperstown was increasingly cut off to him.

The incontrovertible obstacles were financial (Beard I: 23–24). William Cooper had left each of his five sons, in addition to enormous amounts of land, a cash bequest of $50,000, in that day a huge fortune; by 1817 Cooper had spent it all and fallen into debt, as had his brothers. In *The Pioneers,* Cooper disparages the "indolent and comparatively uneducated offspring" of affluent emigrants (30), but it is important to note that Cooper's own overspending was not a matter of dissolute carelessness. It was not his prodigality that consumed his father's legacy, but the unchecked play of his ambition to secure patriarchal stature by establishing his family in a substantial house and by becoming the first farmer of the county. The situation worsened as it became clear that he and his brothers could not settle the outstanding claims on his father's estate. Although they still had large holdings, the depression following 1812 made the land difficult to sell. The full debacle came in 1822 and 1823, when forced sales swept away his remaining land, and even his household goods were seized for an auction Cooper barely stopped.

But as early as Cooper's 1817 departure from Fenimore to visit his father-in-law, the signs of his deracination were unmistakable.

It seems doubtful, however, that the trip away from Cooperstown would have become a twenty-year expatriation without familial pressures as well. Though the problems were relatively minor initially, they moved Cooper toward Westchester and the critical conflict with his father-in-law. When he first transplanted his family to the Fenimore farm in 1813, Cooper anticipated the difficulties his wife would face moving from one of the oldest New York counties to one of the newest. Warned perhaps by his mother's antipathy to the frontier – family legend told of William Cooper having to carry her screaming from their house in Burlington, New Jersey – Cooper acknowledged his wife's close relationship with her father. To ease the difficult break, he commissioned a portrait of John Peter De Lancey for Susan to take to their new home and encouraged his young sisters-in-law to visit often. But the death of their first child, coincident with their move to Cooperstown, could not help but deepen Susan's feelings of isolation in her new situation.

The timing of their 1817 retreat from Cooperstown seems to have been precipitated by a specific family crisis – the loss of both the family's nurse and cook in a single unexpected upheaval. When a recently widowed farmer strayed from the Methodist church, the local deacon swooped down on the Coopers' nurse and persuaded her to redeem the unlikely Brother Blass by marrying him and bringing him back to the true path. In order to care for her new husband, the nurse abruptly left the Coopers and compounded the betrayal by taking along her grown daughter, who had served as the family's cook. Whether or not the story glosses over labor dissatisfaction, Susan Fenimore Cooper remembered her mother's distress at being abandoned and laconically reported that her newborn sister cried for the first three months of her existence.

Any haggard, floor-walking parent can see disaster unfold. With her family far away and no suitable replacement for an experienced nurse to be found, Mrs. Cooper found herself with a four-year-old, a two-year-old, and a colicky baby. Cooper called in a cousin of Mrs. Cooper's for a three-month mission of mercy and comforted his wife with the promise of a visit to her father at Heathcote Hill. But having returned to Westchester, Mrs. Cooper did not risk repetition. By the time she was pregnant with her next child, the decision to stay in Westchester had been made.

The year 1817 also saw the death of Cooper's mother. Although we have very little direct information about the relationship of mother and son, the indirect evidence points steadily to its importance. Not only did Cooper use "Fenimore" to distinguish his land and his own separate identity, he gave her name to his children. Both his first daughter, Elizabeth, and his first son, Fenimore, were matrilineally named. (His wife's mother was also an Elizabeth.) It may have been that Cooper saw something of value in his mother's open distaste for the wilderness. By all accounts, Elizabeth Fenimore Cooper neither forgot, nor allowed anyone else to forget, the crudeness of frontier life, strongly preferring the cultivation of her original home near Philadelphia – as cosmopolitan a city as America then offered. Though Cooper's imaginative involvement with the wilderness obviously transcended his mother's limited view, his accounts of frontier settlement often ridicule the roughness his mother disparaged. They do so humorously, but the shadow of his mother's perspective remains.[7] Though children easily resent the imputations one parent makes against the other, Elizabeth Fenimore Cooper's air of superiority may have given James Cooper some needed leverage against his father. Cultured achievement might offer a route around the giant presence of William Cooper's career.

Initially, the move to Westchester seemed to leave intact Cooper's strategy for gaining authority. To all appearances, he repeated the elements of his life in Cooperstown: he built a new house, joined the Bible and Agricultural societies, and once more became involved in the militia. To this he added a more direct claim to social leadership by working successfully for the gubernatorial campaign of De Witt Clinton. However, he remained in Westchester under terms dictated by the deepest threat to his independence and authority: his failure to measure up in the De Lancey family.

John Peter De Lancey was very close to his eldest daughter

Susan, and though James Cooper's distressed financial situation greatly concerned him, it also offered an opportunity to keep his daughter in closer orbit. He offered his daughter and her husband fifty-seven acres of farm land in Scarsdale, an easy four miles back from Heathcote Hill. No doubt Cooper was relieved to shield his family from the more serious repercussions of his losses, but the terms of the arrangement made perfectly plain that he was in no position to refuse his father-in-law's plan for keeping his daughter near to home, even if he had not been pleased. When Susan Fenimore Cooper described her parents' decision, she noticeably cast it in the passive voice: "It was decided that my father should build a country-house on a farm that was destined for my mother by my grandfather" (35). "It was decided" – barely disguised by that imperious mode, the decision maker was clearly John Peter De Lancey.

The farm was not a gift outright. Expressly to restrict his son-in-law's control, De Lancey drew up a trust: the farm could not be "encumbered or alienated by said James Cooper or subjected to any charge whatever on account of his debts" (*Letters* 1: 87). After the financial debacle at Cooperstown, the son-in-law was placed on familial probation. To salt the wound, De Lancey appointed Susan's brothers as trustees to watch over and pass judgment on Cooper's husbandry and, by implication, on his worthiness to husband Mr. De Lancey's daughter. Thomas was Cooper's exact contemporary; Edward was six years his junior. So hemmed in by De Lanceys, Cooper's tenure at Angevine was conditioned by doubts about his adequacy as a man, husband, and father.

The point is not to make Cooper's father-in-law the villain of the piece, but to emphasize how the De Lanceys' disapproval amplified Cooper's own frustrations. In the court of his own mind, where conviction mattered most, Cooper failed to provide an unquestionably secure livelihood for his growing family. He was now the father of three girls. John Jay had once defined a Federalist in terms reflecting the accepted standards of his native Westchester – standards the De Lanceys and Cooper himself would have shared, despite his more Democratic political leanings. Federalists are "the better sort of people . . . who are orderly and industrious, who are content with their situations and

not uneasy in their circumstances" (Wood 495). Cooper was
neither easy nor content. From the De Lanceys' point of view,
he had certainly proved a bad manager; he might even have
seemed to misrepresent his personal worth at the time of his
engagement (Franklin 18). From Cooper's point of view, the
problem was compounded by the assumed gentility of their expectations. To return to good standing – to a level of stability
and respect that would remove the trust's demeaning provisions
– Cooper had to recoup his fortune. Yet his methods for doing
so, though practiced by a nation of speculators, were abjured
by the De Lanceys.

As a second-generation product of America's expansion to
the frontier, Cooper had developed a social style somewhere
between that of his self-made father and his Tory father-in-law.
But under the pressure of financial collapse, Cooper swung back
to a closer identification with his father. In order to work his
way out of trouble, he adopted William Cooper's aggressive,
speculative strategies. His land investments in the St. Lawrence
valley were risky enough; it takes a good atlas to find De Kalb,
New York, today. But because he had no capital, he went farther
into debt in order to speculate. He pushed his margin as far as
it would go. He bartered his remaining real assets and risked
even the land at Fenimore where he had buried his daughter
(*Letters* 1: 24). And, of course, he incurred still greater distrust
from the De Lanceys.

As the union of a man and woman, James Cooper's marriage
to Susan De Lancey proved wonderfully successful. Their letters
chronicle their interest and affection for each other, and their
easy intimacy. But as a union of families, the marriage was more
problematic. As George Dekker points out, marriage to a De
Lancey was a considerable accomplishment for the young
Cooper, but in terms of his own sense of self, the social match
may have been *too good*. It was an almost Jamesian pairing, with
roles reversed: the scion of a new America brings the fortune
that his rough-edged, self-made father cut out of the wilderness
to the daughter of an aristocratic family that paid for its loyalty
to the old order by forfeiting much of its wealth. However sen-
sible their distrust on practical grounds, the De Lanceys' attitude
toward his speculations cast doubt not only on Cooper himself

but also on his frontier background and that part of his identity tied up with his father.[8]

By 1820, Cooper could no longer endure their judgment on him or the judgment it forced him to make in turn on the gap between his ambitions and accomplishments. He argued openly with his brother-in-law and he began to write. The two were profoundly interrelated. With *Precaution* and *The Spy* behind him, he secured a path to authority independent of his father-in-law. He proceeded to cut off all communication with the De Lanceys and moved to New York. The abrupt move signaled Cooper's firm decision to make writing the foundation of his independent life.

On both sides, the wounds cut deep. Cooper broke the silence between his family and the elder De Lancey at the end of 1822, but the timing and tone of his rapprochement calls into question any real change in his feelings. Cooper's brother-in-law Thomas died of consumption on December 22 (*Letters* 1: 87; SC 50). The next morning, Cooper wrote to offer a truce in polite but somewhat grudging terms. He extended no condolences. He reminded the bereaved De Lancey that he was acting only at the request of his wife, so that she might show her father the tenderness and affection his "age and infirmities require[d]"; he was happy to resume visits between the family, but he required that no mention of their earlier argument be made, either to concede or to explain. His father-in-law agreed, but the chill never left their relationship.

At once bound together and permanently divided by their affection for Susan, John Peter De Lancey and his son-in-law carried on the symbolic gestures of their dispute. Cooper struck out at De Lancey by moving his daughter away from him, not just to Manhattan, but to Europe. In the second year of their tour, Peter De Lancey died. One might say that Cooper took the surest revenge against the authority of a disapproving elder. But when Cooper opened De Lancey's will, he found a document dated January 28, 1823, twelve years after Cooper's marriage and a year after the negotiated truce. Once more De Lancey left all bequests to Susan in trust, the income to be paid to Susan "for her sole and separate use independent of her husband."

Only at Cooper's death would she gain full control of her father's land.

Again in 1820, Cooper's private gestures uncover the strategies of his search for authority. After finishing the manuscript of *Precaution,* Cooper arranged a reading before John Jay and his family. Like the journeys in *Satanstoe,* the finest novel of his late career, Cooper's plan lays out his need for a surrogate family on precise geographic coordinates. From the Coopers' farm at Angevine, John Peter De Lancey's estate lay four miles to the east. Poised on the margin of the Atlantic, Heathcote Hill looked toward England as if bowing to the strong Anglophile allegiances embodied in the De Lanceys' history. The house, with its ancestral name, looked over New Rochelle, where older members of the Huguenot community still descended to the shore in the dark of Sunday mornings and knelt in prayer for a return to France. To the north of Angevine, twenty-five miles into the interior, Governor Jay's house offered an ideal counterpoise to the pressure Cooper felt from his in-laws. Like the De Lanceys, the Jays stood at the top of a Westchester gentry bound together by generations of intermarriages and the shared assumptions of their class. But in terms of their political alignment, the De Lanceys and Jays stood on opposite sides of a deep fissure – the split that made Westchester County a deadly neutral ground during the Revolution. Loyal to the crown, the De Lanceys cast their lot with the old order; supporters of the Revolution, the Jays rose with the New York Whigs who came to prominence after the Revolution (Wood 72, 77). A thirty-year-old Telemachus, Cooper traveled in the spring of 1820 to read his manuscript to the patriarch and his assembled family.

The pilgrimage to the Jays marked out the future direction of Cooper's authorship by returning to reclaimable parts of his past. In this, it illustrates how the basic pattern of Cooper's historical imagination – using the events of the past to judge America's present and future – corresponded to the strategies by which he plotted his own life. At the Jays', Cooper sought approval not merely for the particular manuscript but for his new identity as a writer. William Cooper and John Jay had been Federalist allies during the party's heyday. Although James must have heard his own father discuss Jay's accomplishments, he first experienced Jay's authority for himself within a family context – as the father of William Jay, his closest friend at the small Albany school where they boarded. At the time of his change in careers, he again moved closer to John Jay through his friendship with his sons and their shared political work, a sphere over which the elder Jay inevitably presided.

In seeking Jay's approval, Cooper sought relief from the silent condemnation of his background implicit in the De Lanceys' disapproval of his speculations. Jay had worked with Cooper's father and, in Constitutional debates, had argued without condescension that the public benefited from the "Enterprise, Activity, and Industry of Adventurers" motivated by the "private Love of Gain" (Wood 95–96). John Jay would not carry strong prejudices against the commercial aspects of art, and Cooper's plans as a writer required as much commercial exploitation of his talent as he could possibly negotiate.

But more important, Cooper sought the blessings of a generation that had won high acknowledged authority over the nation *by means of its writing*. John Jay first gained wide recognition as author of "The Address to the People of Great Britain"; in 1777 he drafted the first constitution of New York State and then served as its first chief justice. He negotiated the Treaty of Paris, ending the Revolution, and established his highest claim by joining with Alexander Hamilton and James Madison to write the Federalist Papers. As the first United States chief justice, he wrote important decisions on states' rights, finishing his national career by writing the Jay Treaty, which, though highly unpopular domestically, first established the system of international arbitration (*Britannica* 1972). The political correspondence of his career reads like a directory of the new nation's leaders. John Jay was an acknowledged father of his country; such was the scale of recognition James Cooper sought.

Only in this context can we understand the scope of Cooper's ambitions, the bitterness of his later disappointments, and the tempestuous, self-defeating wrangles with the press and even with his own readership. Though Cooper bristled when reminded of Scott's or Irving's popularity, his ambition transcended literary fame. Literary success gained significance only as it represented public acknowledgment of his social authority. Long after he abandoned his early plan of writing a historical novel for each of the original colonies, Cooper's ambition remained to attain the stature of the Madisons, Jeffersons, and Jays.

As the surrogate father of Cooper's literary career, John Jay would allow Cooper to join cultured achievement to the intense activity and public engagement so characteristic of William Cooper. Although the imitative quality of his first novel hid the bold nature of his national ambitions and the extent of his alignment with patriarchal authority, the next three works document that his art was empowered by his often conflicted filial identification with the founders of his life and country. John Jay specifically recommended the story of *The Spy* as a tale suitable for fiction; Cooper took the paternal gift and transformed it into a story of an unrelated but "true" son winning recognition from the nation's father. *The Pioneers* looks back to his own father's claim as a founder; *The Pilot* returns to the naval authority Cooper knew as a sailor during his passage from adolescence into manhood and the maverick role John Paul Jones played in the country's paternity. Both the thematic consistency of these novels and the remarkable speed of Cooper's production demonstrate the breakthrough of Cooper's frustrated energies sponsored by his new alignment with the Jays (Dekker 13–15).

The trip to Bedford also repeated an earlier experiment in identity involving William Jay, himself a prolific writer on agriculture, religion, abolition, and international law (*Letters* 1: 30). William Jay and James Cooper had been classmates, when only eleven, at the small boarding school of the Reverend Thomas Ellison in Albany. In the classic English pattern, their lessons required memorizing Virgil's Eclogues. Away from family and, in the purest Virgilian sense, from *patria,* William and James entertained the other boarders at night by reciting Virgil through the darkness.

At that age and place, such recitations say less of academic virtue than of incipient adolescent *virtù.* They represent a kind of theft from the adult world. Lessons that satisfy the authority of Rev. Ellison during the day become, through the clandestine passage of prohibited after-hours, the stuff of autonomous juvenile selves. At that same time, Cooper first discovered that his literary imagination could win the respect of his peers. When Virgil waned, Cooper invented romances to entertain his fellows. This was in 1801–02. The journey to the Jays took Cooper back to an obviously immature, but nevertheless valued, sense of self.

Of his various attempts to reverse the disastrous financial losses of his first decade as husband and father, James Beard calls Cooper's first venture into writing the "most quixotic experiment of all." In the sense that America offered little hope of reward to a novelist, Beard is certainly correct. As Charles Brockden Brown's flash across the literary sky made clear, even speculations like Cooper's in frontier real estate and whaling ships must have seemed gold in the vault beside the prospects of a writer. But if we are to judge by Cooper's wholehearted commitment and by his understanding of how writing could satisfy his ambitions, there was little that was quixotic about it. By 1820, he conceived of writing explicitly as a route to authority: "Books . . . are, in a great measure, the instruments of controlling the opinions of a nation like ours. They are an engine alike powerful to save or destroy" (Beard xxii). Control and power were what Cooper wanted, and the first months of his career show how determined he was to get it. As George Dekker observed, by the time Cooper finished *Precaution* he was "an already addicted author" (18). If there was anything at all whimsical in his experiment, it was his attempt to cover the totality of his commitment behind the transparent pretense that the work read to the Jay family had been written by an English cousin of Mrs. Cooper's.

Although it might seem a dilettante's effort to shrug off responsibility, Cooper's initial secrecy was, in fact, an unlikely attempt to secure a retreat from a game played for the highest psychic stakes. The pose is betrayed in his first letter of inquiry to the publisher Andrew Thompson Goodrich. Initially the letter pretends to self-effacing casualness:

> Dear Sir – The arrangements for the late election and the subsequent death of the Mother of Mrs. Cooper having compelled

> me to remain at home for the last two or three months – For
> the double purpose of employment and the amusement of my
> wife in her present low spirits – I commenced the writing of
> a moral tale. (1: 41–42)

In the syntax of these lines, the author appears first as a diminutive direct object ("me") subject to the compulsion of events. Cooper must wait for the intervention of four additional explanatory prepositional phrases before taking center stage as "I." But by the end of the letter, all casualness is gone. He hints at a meeting with Goodrich, underscoring the need for secrecy with comic insistence – "if you are disposed to a ride or a sail I should be happy to see you – (of course without mentioning where you go) – to spend a Sunday here." Across the top of the letter he scrawled, "Most-Strictly confidential" (1: 41–43; Lyman 19: 221–22).

On the second of July he explained that he wished to remain anonymous to save disgrace. Ten days later he again insisted: "take care of my *name,* and do not let it appear in any manner." Melodramatically emphasizing the need for secrecy, he replaced his own name in the signature with the title of the book, again underscored, "Yours & – 'Precaution' " (7/12/20 Beard 49). He coupled his warning with a further bizarre caution to wrap the proofs more carefully lest someone at the Mamaroneck post office expose his cover. Cooper's snappish tone, edged with paranoia, strikes a note heard throughout his literary correspondence. Yet readers of the Leatherstocking tales and of the novels of frontier settlement know by heart Cooper's insistence that names be earned and correspond to the innermost value of the self. To Cooper, the packages of manuscript and proof shuttling between Angevine and Manhattan were, to borrow from Emerson, part and parcel of his identity (Franklin 23).

In addition, the escalating epistolary bombardment Cooper launched at his printer illustrates his immediate shift into a professional mode, unusual in a first novelist and not at all in line with his pose as an amateur. He immediately assumed the aggressive stance that steeled his resolve through great successes and extended droughts and made him America's first career novelist. Although he recognized the weakness of his first effort, he wanted *Precaution* rushed through the press: "as it is a highly moral book, . . . I believe it will sell" (1: 48). He no sooner contacted the printer than he began to hound him with questions about advertisements. By August, he had offered $200 "to stimulate" his efforts and demanded more proof pages. By September, he had already taken up the issue of English sales and protested his bookseller's plan to offer large discounts. By October, he had taken charge of directing review copies to favorably disposed friends.

The same series of letters to Goodrich discloses a precocious confidence in his literary power. On the last day of May, 1820, Cooper serenely promised that, since writing was going well, he would finish the last third of *Precaution,* a full British volume, in two weeks. By June 12, he had done so – a day ahead of schedule and at the rate of a chapter a day. Without pause, he began *The Spy.* Though still shielding his commitment by crediting the new project to the "persuasion of Mrs. Cooper," he amassed nearly sixty 800-word manuscript pages by June 28 (Beard 44). Nor was his confidence limited to productivity. In his complaints about the silent "corrections" and errors of the printers, Cooper speaks with an easy authority, unusual in a neophyte, about his taste in literary style: "There is no grosser error in style than the affected personification of such kind of things – it distinguishes the Della Cruscan School and God forbid it should creep into any of my pages" (Beard I: 56).

In its sheer volume, its unrelenting pace, its eye for the commercial value of his "moral tale," Cooper's correspondence recalls William Cooper's voracious involvement in his world. For the first time, James Cooper found a vocation to tap the energy and opportunistic drive of his true paternal legacy.

Writing had solved the crisis in his sense of self-worth, and the true nature of the solution surfaces in a casual remark about his wife's preference for those first pages of *The Spy:* "my female Mentor says it throws *Precaution* far in the back-ground – I confess I am more partial to this new work myself as being a Country-man and perhaps a younger child" (Beard 44). On the one hand, his reference to the new work as a younger child reveals the paternal relationship he assumed toward his literary issue. As his progeny, literature will connect him to the society and to the future. For Cooper, that avenue to authority was essential to a credible identity. On the other hand, his own cautious identification with the fledgling book reveals his lingering sense of himself as a younger son. By achieving what had not been expected of him, his books will finally win acknowledgment for the unrecognized "younger child" of William Cooper and give him independence from the unwanted authority of his father-in-law. With the publication of *Precaution* in the autumn, the journey Cooper undertook to the Jays circled to completion; answering William Jay's praise for the published work, Cooper wrote that he at last felt "understood" (1: 66; Dekker 13–14).

Several practical considerations supported his change in careers. Over the more overt claims to political authority that Cooper had been making as a supporter of De Witt Clinton, writing enjoyed an advantage. At some level Cooper may have sensed that a man of his political views would necessarily operate in the shadow of the great Federalist founders. If his politics at this time had been radically different in content or even in style, as Jackson's had been a decade later, political success might have delivered him the authority he desired. But as it was, his beliefs too often echoed those of the previous generation, and the unpopular side of those positions as well. He could not carve a new trail and openly express distrust of human nature and "the Virtue and good Sense of the People" as Washington and Jay had done at the time of the Confederation (qtd. in Wood 425, 471–72). In Cooper's severe self-judgment, gains in the political sphere would have reaffirmed his status as son rather than crediting his fatherhood.

Furthermore, Cooper's political career was based in his father-in-law's backyard; moreover, it became clear, after the frustrating months of correspondence over the proof pages of *Precaution,* that writing would require a move to Manhattan. Before 1820, Cooper's position in society had depended less on his own achievement than on the hierarchical rank of the Coopers and De Lanceys: in Westchester, his dependence was physically represented by living on family property. For the thirteen years following his move to New York, Cooper lived always as a renter. His preeminence would not hang on the vertical connections of family, but rather would be sustained by the horizontal support of a large, buoying public. Initially a matter of necessity, it became the pattern of his life and corresponded to his confidence in his position as a writer. Later, when he felt that American society had withdrawn the support necessary to his sense of self, he reasserted his family connections and returned to live on family property at Cooperstown.

Above all, the move to New York brought him into close and frequent contact with a large group of male friends from whom he chiefly derived his new sense of horizontal support, based on his position among the members of his own generation. In her memoirs, Susan Fenimore Cooper remembers her family's house as a thoroughfare of her father's friends, those from his navy connections intermingling with a newer group of artists and writers. The publication of *Precaution* brought Cooper into the literary circle that gathered at Wiley's book shop at 3 Wall Street (1: 24). He grew closer to the group as a contributor to Charles K. Gardner's quarterly *The Literary and Scientific Repository and Critical Review* (1820–22) and, after his move to New York, founded the Bread and Cheese, a club where his mixed group of friends hosted one another at the house of Abigail Jones, the Delmonico's of an earlier era (SC 50). As Beard notes, "Cooper with his brash assertiveness and boundless creativity was ideally qualified to provide leadership" to a rough and opportunistic New York that badly wanted culture (Beard 83). In New York's mixture of commercial energy and unfinished crudeness there persisted frontier contradictions akin to those of Cooper's Templeton.

Two opposed recollections of the young writer illustrate the part these friendships played in Cooper's strategy for establishing independent authority. Dr. John W. Francis, a member of the Bread and Cheese, particularly emphasized Cooper's chameleonlike adaptability to the different manners of his male friends:

> It was gratifying to observe the dexterity with which Mr. Cooper would cope with some Eastern friend who contributed to our delight with a "Boston notion," or with Trelawny, the associate of Byron, descanting on Greece and the "Younger Son," or with any guests of the club, however dissimilar their habits or character; accommodating his conversation and manners with the most marvellous facility. (1: 83–84)

In a writer who made inflexibility so important a part of his persona after his return to America in the 1830s, this adaptability seems hardly credible. But as his later inflexibility mirrored his sense of isolation, so his accommodation at an earlier stage demonstrates his need to buttress his newly independent sense of self by binding himself to his peers. The almost unconscious mimicry of the manners and tone of his interlocutors offers a glimpse, in a public context, of an imagination that could comprehend the divergent auras of Judge Temple and Natty Bumppo. On the other hand, William Cullen Bryant remembers Cooper "holding forth" and was startled by Cooper's lack of modesty: "Mr. Cooper engrossed the whole conversation and seemed a little giddy with the great success his works have met with." Though seemingly opposed to Dr. Francis's recollection, Bryant's vignette exposes a crucial second step in Cooper's unconscious strategy. As founder of the Bread and Cheese, Cooper first created a society of peers to support his move into a new career. On this more egalitarian field he then exercised his newly achieved authority as a writer – an authority independent of the generational lines dominating his familial experience, but still setting him high.

Bryant keenly saw an edge of arrogance – an overplayed attempt to shelter a long-besieged self-confidence. Cooper's self-importance would later harden into a less attractive, sometimes self-destructive public stance. But at this transitional point in his life, both his braggadocio and his warm friendships should be understood as the means for sustaining a final break with those earlier strategies to achieve patriarchal authority associated with his father's past and with the land. One morning at 3 Beech Street, Cooper walked into his wife's parlor and, without speaking, handed her a newspaper and then left the room (SC 52). At Cooperstown, the house of his patriarchal design had burned to the ground. From now on, his claims to patriarchal authority would rest not on the "Fenimore" built of stone over Lake Otsego but on the "Fenimore" flourished by his pen.

Like Stephen Crane at the end of the century, Cooper enjoyed a meteoric rise to national fame with the publication of his second novel. Artists and dramatists immediately transposed *The Spy* onto canvas and stage, signaling both Cooper's responsiveness to his culture and his influence upon it. After that success, the entire first edition of *The Pioneers* sold out on the morning of its publication. In acknowledgment of his achievement, the American Philosophical Society made him a member in April of 1823; Columbia College gave him an honorary degree in 1824; on the eve of his departure for Europe, his friends hailed him at a testimonial dinner, and the city awarded its silver medal "as a testimony of their high respect for [him], as a Citizen of the United States, who, by his writings, has added to the glory of the Republic" (1: 84). By the time Cooper suffered the loss of his house and land, writing had brought him what he needed when he set out to the Jays with his moral tale in 1820.

3

Negotiating a Place in the Patriarchy: Literary Style and the Transfer of Power

For writers, stylistic experimentation leading to a distinct and authentic voice is in some way the professional equivalent of an earlier passage into adulthood. In Cooper's case that equivalence becomes particularly clear in *The Pioneers;* not only are Cooper's shifting stylistic strategies unusually distinct and the line of development more boldly charted, but the experiments in tone and point of view focus on the fictional portrayal of his own father. In *A World Elsewhere,* Richard Poirier defines a distinctive American style more intent on displacing existing environments than on negotiating with them or criticizing them. Although *The Pioneers* is threaded with defiance, its style achieves the power to release Cooper and his readers into a world of his own making, not so much by turning its back on his father's frontier world as by a strategy for subsuming the father's power into the son's art (Poirier 3–16). In the course of *The Pioneers,* Cooper's style negotiates a series of different relationships between the narrator, the reader, and Judge Temple. In Cooper's shift from the descriptive impulse, motivated by his longing for the Cooperstown of his youth, to the masterful symbolic drama of the central scenes, we can trace a two-step progression as his interest in establishing a point of view independent of his father unfolds into a full-scale assumption of authority in his own right.

Cooper's reliance on writing as a way of negotiating his relationship to authority antedates his sudden decision to become a novelist. In later years of prolific output, Cooper evidently enjoyed the irony of looking back to the time when he had confessed himself much "averse to writing" (1: 26). His distaste became a family joke that Susan Fenimore Cooper wryly repeated in her 1861 account of her father's first attempts as a novelist:

> Hitherto no man could have shown himself farther from any inclination for authorcraft. He was not one of those people who like the feeling of foolscap, the sight of pen and ink, who indulge secret partialities for note-books, diaries and extracts. His portfolio was wholly empty. (17)

Yet these jokes are misleading. Letters remain from those early years, and though they are few, Cooper's difficulty with writing argues less for casual dismissal than for attention to those impulses sufficiently strong to overcome his natural aversion to pen and ink. The stronger the aversion, the more extraordinary must have been his need to write on the specific occasion marked by each letter. Cooper's youthful style, often inconsistent and uncertain, confesses at least as much about his standing in his family as do the texts themselves. Cooper's early correspondence establishes the important relationship between stylistic strategies and his desire to control and assume the power of male authority.

Of the twelve extant letters written before his marriage, six were addressed to the Department of the Navy and six to his father and older brothers Richard and Isaac. Especially after their father's death, these two young men stood, or tried to stand, in a quasi-paternal relationship to their much younger brother. Fed by misunderstandings over orders and financial accounts, the letters to *five* secretaries of the navy continued twelve years beyond his two years of active service. Interesting as harbingers of Cooper's public persona, the official correspondence follows a pattern of petition and defiance clearly originating in and more fully revealed by the more intimate relationships played out in the family letters. Analyzing the letters of an unformed boy requires a certain good-humored suspension of skepticism, but rough and incomplete as these documents are, they offer rare, if oblique, insight into the pattern of family relationships that the letters of Cooper's young manhood make explicit.

In the earliest letter, James Cooper strives to make contact with the father whose absence from home inspired the ten-year-old's struggle with orthography and grammar:

CoopersTown March 3, 1800

Dear Papa

    I take this opportunity to write to you as Isaac is a going directly to Philadelphia. We have got 6 lambs one has died and another is most dead. Mr. Macdonnal'd is a going to leave us for Albany. Mama will not let Samuel go with Isaac though he wished to very much. I go to school to Mr. Cory where I write and Cypher. Mr. Macdonol'd has had a new student from New York who encamped in Mr. Kents barn and laid 3 days there without being found out and had his feet frozen. We are all well. I hope I shall have the pleasure of receiveing a letter from you soon as this letter reaches you –

      Your

        affectionate

           son

JAMES K. (sic) COOPER

       18 century 1800

Clearly Mr. Cory had his work cut out for him, yet the note speaks with Huck-like authenticity. Cooper's ear picks up the local dialect – "is a going"; his direct phrasing – "one has died and another is most dead" – flashes a boy's morbid wonder before the reader. Yet the heart of the letter's charm lies in the immediacy of the father's presence to the mind of the boy. Unselfconscious in his greeting – "Papa," not father – he quickly dispenses with the formality required to announce an unusual event – a letter from the youngest of his five sons – and proceeds to the news from "CoopersTown." He knows what his father wants to hear. As the letter moves without pause from family to farm to village, back to the family, and once more out to the village, its structure captures the integration of family and community. In the boy's mind, no clear demarcation separates the different spheres; they are all of equal concern to the patriarch and his "affectionate son."

    To the boy, the gruesome mystery of the student with frozen feet seems particularly worthy of attention. Extending his longest sentence phrase after phrase, James Cooper makes his first narrative foray to give his father pleasure. The father's vivid presence becomes even clearer when the boy hurries to reassure his absent parent that "We are all well." As he brings the letter to a close, a certain self-consciousness comes in. The language becomes more formal as he more directly enunciates the purpose of his letter. In requesting "the pleasure of receiveing [*sic*] a letter from you soon as this letter reaches you," the boy discloses that he misses his father. He writes to bring himself closer to William Cooper and to win from him a token of his affection in return.

Cooper's sense of his place within the family further emphasizes his need to make contact with his father. The letter openly recognizes the significant distinction between older and younger brothers: Isaac and Richard, respectively eight and fourteen years older than James, can participate in the business of their father; younger children like Samuel and himself cannot and must remain at home under their mother's command. In later letters, Cooper chafed at this sense of his brothers' precedence, and even at ten his desire to share their access to his father may be at work in his striking assumption of a middle initial in his signature: "your affectionate son James K. Cooper." Beard explains that Cooper's sense of admiration for his father's legal clerk and secretary Moss Kent "was so great that he temporarily adopted the middle initial 'K.'" A child's experimentation with different names shows an increasing self-consciousness about identity, and, in this case, serves notice of an incipient sense of his control over the alliances that support independent selfhood. Certainly the "K" calls out for attention in a writer so bent on adopting Fenimore and who so often exploited the idea of surrogate fathers to formulate his ideas of historical change in his fiction. In another context it might be tempting to see Cooper's new initial as an effort to challenge his father with his preference for Kent, and at some level that may inform the self-conscious mark. But coming from a boy keenly aware of his place as the youngest child, it seems more likely that the "K" was another strategy for approaching his father. By joining the name of Judge Cooper's clerk to his own, he symbolically assumed the status of someone like Richard or Isaac who worked with his father. At this point, the surrogate represented access, not substitution.

As Cooper moved into adolescence and gained limited control over his writing, he no longer permitted his readers the open, unscreened access to his thoughts and affections. Money became the object of his correspondence, and in exploiting the honorable tradition of the letter home, Cooper learned that letter-writing could temporarily recast his relationship to his father and brother. Though he still assumed a very junior status in the family, he was able and, for the time being, willing to manipulate it.

In an 1801 letter to his older brother Isaac, then storekeeper at Cooperstown, James buries his fear of having displeased his father at the center of a note he had been asked to write about a purchase of cambric muslin:

> Sisters & Papa left this, this morning. Papa gave me 70 dollars for to pay some debts and as I went to Mr. Banyers to see them start I either lost them a going or after I came to Mr. Banyers I do not know which. I searcht [*sic*] for them but they have not yet shown their faces, Sisters both where [*sic*] in good health, likewise Papa . . . you must excuse mistakes bad writing as I am in a great hurry.

Seventy dollars was a large amount for a boy to carry, and the nervous extension of the long sentence with the repetitions of "I" show his real anxiety about the loss. But after the awkward full stop at "which," he seems to recoup his resources. Having flattered his twenty-year-old brother by addressing him by his rank in the militia, he calls on his skills as a raconteur to enlist the "corporal" to his cause; by personifying the dollars ("they have not yet shown their faces"), he charmingly displaces responsibility. While his confession makes light of a large mistake, its self-conscious charm hopes to anticipate and dissipate the force of his father's judgment by recruiting the support of his brother's seniority.

By mid-adolescence, Cooper wrote to his father with a degree of formality in noticeable contrast to this first experiment. The letter's purpose was to request money in order to settle a large debt to a tavern keeper with the Dickensian appellation of Mr. Mix; the purpose of its tone was to distance himself as far as possible from his own financial mess and to divert his father's wrath. After an illegible salutation, the damaged manuscript continues:

. . . as M. Mix is very desirous of his money being about to
go to New York. If you have any and if it is agreeable to you
to pay You would I believe much oblige him. I have not a
copper of money and am much in want of a little.

I am your affectionate

Son

JAMES COOPER

By taking on a breezy, businesslike tone older than his fifteen
years might allow, Cooper manages to make his debts seem
exclusively an affair between Mr. Mix and his father. He succeeds in placing himself as tangentially as possible: he *believes*
his father would oblige Mr. Mix. Furthermore, the boy's style
has become more flexible; he can vary his tone according to the
different strategies he adopts to manage his father. After hiding
himself during the requested debt settlement, the boy drops the
stance of gazetteer-accountant and, needing money, slides into
the informality of the young collegiate attempting quick charm
to earn his "copper."

The complexity of Cooper's relationship to authority reveals
itself far more completely in two later letters to his oldest brother
Richard dated only three weeks apart. Written after his experience before the mast, these letters offer unusual evidence of a
youth's developing sense of manhood. Though the letters skirt
the specific occasion of wounded feelings, the two brothers evidently argued over the degree of authority James should yield
to a brother fourteen years his elder. In his professional capacity
as a midshipman recently recommended for his first promotion,
James Cooper felt he could claim his place as a man, but within
the family he remained the youngest brother and that unchanged
status threatened a vaunted, but obviously tender, sense of self.
Cooper wrote to subdue the subordinate and inferior self-image
reflected back at him by his family. He signed the first letter
"Your Friend and Brother," but the apposition of the two terms
comes after a struggle; although Cooper wishes to make them
equivalent conveyors of good will, between these two brothers
the two words comprehend opposed relationships: to be a friend
is to be equal; to be a brother is to be subordinate, unmanly, a
boy.

The first letter is striking for what it leaves out. Although he
clearly had no other reason for writing, Cooper could not bring

himself to address the conflict with his brother directly. Six short paragraphs jump from one thing to the next without sustaining any of the ostensible subjects for more than a few lines. Obviously hesitant, even fearful, about confronting his older brother, Cooper used the letter to scout out the ground – to reconnoiter different approaches to Richard's authority with as little exposure to direct fraternal fire as possible.

Moving quickly away from the stiff formality of his "My Dear Sir" greeting, Cooper tried to assume a tone of easy good fellowship that would set him on an equal footing with his brother. But his inner sense of their disparity betrayed him and the effort was strained. The intended breeziness comes across as too abrupt and even slightly cocky: "You and I are old acquaintances, but new correspondents. If you don't think fit to answer this letter why – I shan't think fit to write another" (1: 10). Jocularity barely disguises his acknowledgment that Richard can undermine his younger brother simply by ignoring him. And as the broken structure of the sentence suggests, the comfort of retaliation in kind is meager at best: Richard does not need James's acknowledgment; James does need Richard's.

Through the scattered paragraphs that follow, James's tone carries his message. His manly cheerfulness savors rumors of war and longs for "the pleasure of seeing salt water once more." As if to fight off the unmentioned argument and his brother's disapproval, he emphasizes that part of his experience that gives credence to his maturity in the world outside the family. But after pumping himself up, his preoccupation with his stature in his brother's eyes reasserts itself in the longest paragraph of the letter:

> I have purchased a brace of pistols for twenty dollar[s?] which I shall keep in remembrance of your Friendship. There is no prospect of my having occasion to use them in this quarter of the world. I shall remember your injunctions – whenever I may have occasion of that kind – . . . (1: 10)

By moving in two directions at once, the paragraph defines the horns of his dilemma. On the one hand, purchasing weapons of honor flamboyantly asserts a claim to manhood whether his older brother likes it or not. On the other hand, he retreats from the gesture as soon as he announces it, assuring his elder sibling that he will not use them and that, if he does, he will follow his injunctions. He confirms what he set out to defy: his familial status as Richard's protégé. On a more covert level, the double impulse is repeated by the ambiguity of his intention to keep the pistols "in remembrance of your Friendship." The declared tribute is challenged by the dubious psychological possibilities of commemorating a tense relationship with a sibling of nearly paternal superiority with a pair of deadly dueling pistols.

In the second letter to Richard, these ambiguities play themselves out more frankly; each of the three paragraphs has a clearly differentiated tone and the signaled shifts in attitude plot a drama of deference and defiance. Cooper's maneuvering affords a rough analogy to Hawthorne's study of young Robin Molineux's relationship to authority in "My Kinsman, Major Molineux." In that story Hawthorne repeatedly calls attention to Robin's self-conscious efforts to compose his speech and features in hopes of presenting a bearing at once respectful and manly – efforts at repression and posing that break apart in his irrepressible shout of laughter at his elder kinsman.

Encouraged by Richard's quick reply to his first letter, Cooper feels emboldened to address their disagreement more openly and at greater length:

> My Dear Sir
>   I received your letter by the last mail, to your offer of continuing the correspondence I accede with great pleasure – Your advice will always be regarded as that, of an <u>elder Brother</u> – Family dissensions are ever to me disagreeable – If any have or should take place in which I should be unfortunate enough to participate – it would always be my ardent wish to bury them in oblivion – could it be done consistent with my own honor, and that of my family – The ebullitions of <u>my</u> youth, will I hope be forgotten. They have afforded me a lesson by which I may hereafter profit – I flatter myself your caution on this subject was unnecessary. <u>Nature</u> will <u>predominate</u> – I am convinced that no connection will ever break the ties of blood – I write freely for I am writing to a <u>Brother</u> – . . .
>   (1: 12)

Obviously, this is meant to be conciliatory; he apologizes for an indiscretion over which the two brothers have argued and bows to the superior status of his "<u>elder Brother</u>." Yet he concedes only with the greatest difficulty. Each accommodation spurs him to a counterclaim. He would bury earlier dissensions "could it be done consistent with my own honor, and that of my family" – a caveat that asserts both his independence and his significant stature within the family. Having submitted to Richard's advice, he dismisses it as unnecessary. Furthermore, his strained efforts to generalize the particular and personal conflict and to distance himself from his "youth," his legalistic caution ("if any have or should take place"), and his retreat into cliché all suggest that he needed to summon considerable energy in order to repress the impulse toward rebellion.

Although the reconciliation has taken effort, Cooper seems to feel he has set the record straight. In the paragraph's final line, the elder Brother, earlier underscored to describe Richard's role as advisor, has been shortened to Brother in a closing that emphasizes their equality. That achievement releases Cooper's manly social identity from the problematic inferiority of his family status and the second paragraph launches into a long exuberance over preparations for the threatened war with Great Britain. Unchecked by any of the formal constrictions of the earlier paragraph, Cooper's prose concludes with notable bluster: "The British officers we are told are warm – if they attack us some of them may be eventually cold – Woolsey [Cooper's commander] is a fine firm fellow, and would fight the Brig to the last extremity" (1: 12).

Once released from the paternal aspect of his brother's authority, however, Cooper's rebelliousness silently reasserts itself. As Robin Molineux succumbs to the contagious spirit of the chaotic rebel parade, so Cooper gives himself over to his own exultant contemplations of military manhood. In the third and final paragraph of the letter, Cooper swaggers into a brotherly freedom of discourse at which Richard must have paled. James had heard the news of scandal between Richard's wife and another man, and, like Robin Molineux, he could not resist the urge to ridicule the shame of his elder kinsman: "I shall be along your way shortly accompanied by two gentlemen, one of the navy the other of the army – both fine young men – I hope we shan't take the lady of Apple Hill in the straw. I write plain" (1: 12). In no uncertain terms, Cooper knocks the "elder Brother" from the saddle of his accustomed dignity. The jaunty informality, the confident assertion of the first person, the exuberant appositions celebrating the virility of Cooper and his companions, the break in decorum of drawing a cartoon of a haystack around the word "straw," all bespeak release from constraint as loudly as Robin's laugh. Cooper quickly closes his letter, "I am your Brother," and it is clearly in the final subversive cast of the relationship with Richard, rather than in the ostensible reconciliation, that Cooper takes the most satisfaction.

The early letters of his marriage show a marked change. Writing to his wife, Cooper drops both the ingratiating formality and the defiance that marked his relationship to authority both in his family and in his long negotiations with the navy over furloughs and accounts. By giving him authority within a family of his own, his marriage to Susan reconciled his earlier sense of conflict between manhood in the world and his junior status in his father's family. Significantly, he admits for the first time "feeling a degree of pleasure" in writing (1: 26). To complete more than thirty volumes over a period of as many years, Cooper must have sustained both the compulsion to write and the satisfaction in the act of writing. That satisfaction came from successfully negotiating with the authority that challenged him in order to achieve a position from which he could assert his own.

The letters to his wife reverse the economic equation of the early letters to father and brothers, where his dependent position revealed itself in his efforts to cajole money from his elders. He urges his wife to take money from him and, betraying the masculine cultural profit in enforcing women's economic dependence, he openly relishes the confirmation of his independence that generosity affords him:

> I send you Forty Dollars which will make about Seventy in the whole – if this should not be enough you will write to me without reserve – If there is any thing I have a right to complain of in your conduct as a wife it is in too much hesitation in applying for that portion of your pecuniary supplies which is to be more particularily applied to your own use . . . I would have you always apply to me without the least reserve, and would also have you believe that the spending of no mon-

ey is more pleasant to me than that which contributes to your comfort – I will enclose you more before I come down – you can then use it as you want it or not. (1: 31)

This close association of his financial status with the conflict of dependent and independent self-images sheds further light on Cooper's vulnerability to the loss of his father's fortune and the general economic collapse of his twenties and early thirties. In addition to the real practical threat to his family's livelihood and well-being, the losses threatened to return him to the role of petitioner, and according to the patterns of his early writing, that role condemns him once again to the status of youngest son.

When Cooper reviewed *The Pioneers* for the 1832 edition, he apologized for the autobiographical impulse that had led him away from the "general picture . . . to describe scenes, and perhaps he may add characters, that were so familiar to his own youth" (Beard ed. 6). "Too fastidious attention to originals" would destroy the charm of fiction and even at the first publication he had classified his novel as "A Descriptive Tale" to forewarn readers and preempt their disappointment. During the lengthy opening third of the novel, accounting for the state of Judge Temple's family and the village to which he has given his name, little plot develops, and even the magnificent thematic tensions of the opening chapter long run fallow. Yet the artistic difficulties posed by "attention to originals" and Cooper's solutions offer a remarkable field for study. Like the awkwardness of the early letters, Cooper's marked stylistic experiments reveal a passage to maturity. In *The Pioneers,* his efforts to establish his authority as a writer converge with efforts to come to terms with his father's originality – a term loaded for Cooper with its full complement of significance. To present his father as Marmaduke Temple in *The Pioneers,* Cooper had to grapple with William Cooper's manifold preeminence – his originality as the source of his son's life and position, as a larger-than-life personality, as a frontier founder.

The progress of those grapplings is recorded in the stylistic shift from the long descriptive account in the book's opening third to the structured progression of the increasingly symbolic central scenes. Looking back on the novel, Cooper recognized the "temptation to delineate that which he had known rather than that which he might have imagined," but in practice the known and the imagined are not such neatly separable alternatives (Beard ed. 6). The stylistic development of *The Pioneers* suggests that the real struggle in writing about scenes and characters familiar to his youth was not to avoid the known, but *to transform* the known of his father's world into the imagined of his.

The stylistic changes turn on Cooper's experiments with narrative point of view and particularly on the problem of how to approach his father's stature. As he shifts his approach, the novel moves from a descriptive to a more symbolic mode; the characters, originally seen as representative of a specific frontier demography at a particular historical moment, take on larger significance as representatives of persisting cultural forces; and readers, initially safely distanced from the action, are drawn closer to the experience and imperfect vision of the characters. Finding solutions to the problem of narrating the life of the family patriarch released the full synecdochic power of the frontier romance.

The opening scene of *The Pioneers* faces the reader with Marmaduke Temple's power. Cooper marks the latent force of his physical presence even before he asserts the claims of his wealth and social position. Wrapped in abundant fur against the winter cold, Temple initially announces himself to the reader by his "large stature"; the eyes, promising "extraordinary intellect, covert humor, and great benevolence" appear only to the closer view, and then through the "mask" of his fur hat. We learn that the figure underneath the greatcoat is the widowed father of the young woman beside him, but before identifying him by name, Cooper rushes us into the vortex of his masculine impulsiveness. Stirred by the baying of Leatherstocking's hound, the patriarch follows the same instinct that later tempts Natty to cut the throat of a swimming buck and that D. H. Lawrence identified as that of a killer. The man beneath the "mask" stands erect, throws aside the garments that kept him from our full view, scrambles for his gun, "and with a practised eye and steady

hand, drew a trigger [and] turned [the gun's] muzzle towards
his intended victim and fired again" (16). Even before we discover that the shot has wounded Oliver Edwards, we know the
patriarch as a man of explosive and possibly threatening energy;
by its unblinking association with the fowling piece, that energy
is coded as masculine and sexual.

By postponing the history of Marmaduke Temple's rise to
wealth and social position until the second chapter, Cooper
temporarily disassociates the particular code words that Temple
employs to mark his authority from their social basis and ties
them instead to his boasts as a hunter. In his exhilaration, Temple
carelessly, if good-humoredly, debases his claims to the slain
deer by insisting on that "honor" when only a moment earlier
he had confessed to Natty, "I hardly think I struck him" (17).
The Judge enjoys bringing in legal terms for their effect: "the
shot in the heart was unnecessary – what we call an act of su-
pererogation, Leatherstocking" (21). The words tilt the scales
in his favor by calling up his authority as judge. Although from
the outside readers can enjoy the evident relish Marmaduke takes
in disputation for its own sake, Natty registers the pressure latent
in Marmaduke's good humor; in his cranky way, Natty identifies the underlying premise that authority rests squarely on
power – "that might often makes right here, as well as in the
old country, for what I can see" (18).

In the fourth chapter, when Temple's servants and friends
come out to greet the approaching sleigh and "gaping women
and children . . . thronged the windows to witness the arrival
of their landlord and his daughter," Cooper establishes the public's relationship to Temple's patriarchal stature (66). But the
opening scene suggests the more complex ambiguities of Cooper's private effort to find a comfortable relationship to William
Cooper's power. The narrative proposes two opposed alternatives; in a way it anticipates the balanced irony of *The Wept
of Wish-Ton-Wish,* but it does so, as we might expect in a first
attempt by a younger novelist, in rawer, more emotional terms.

On the one hand, the narrative offers the possibility of drawing as close as possible to the patriarch. In a novel where Cooper
himself is returning to the scene of his childhood, he moves in
the first paragraphs to evoke the filial piety of "the son, who,

born in the land, piously wishes to linger around the grave of his father" (10). The emotional power of this alternative enters the narrative in the relationship of Elizabeth Temple to her father. In a book that celebrates so many of the details of William Cooper's life, the reduction in the size of the family stands out. Still suffering the consequences of a decade of financial disaster in which his share of William Cooper's fortune could not support the responsibilities left him by his four indebted and now deceased older brothers, Cooper imagines a father who "had but one child" as heir to inherit his wealth and property (39). Obviously there are other imaginable sources for this configuration; Wayne Franklin effectively argues that the unusual closeness of Cooper's wife and father-in-law informs this relationship and some of the frustration of Oliver Edwards as well (106). But the closeness of daughter and father, signaling not so much the desire to identify with the patriarch's power as the desire to draw close to it, also re-creates the impulse we saw in Cooper's earliest letter to remove the distance between father and offspring.

Establishing a contrast to this affectionate model of the family, the opening scene gives at least as much attention to Oliver Edwards and his inexpressible anger at Judge Temple. Though the eventual uncovering of his Effingham ancestry offers one sort of explanation for his anger, the "facts" are delayed until very late in the novel and, in any case, do not fully account for his flushed silence on the subject of his wrongs. Cooper brushes dangerously close to absurdity by repeating on a number of occasions the picture of his wild gestures and inarticulate rantings. Clearly, the dominant impression is the depth of the anger and the necessity of repressing its true source.

Although cast as an accident, the wounding of Oliver Edwards in the opening scene points to the sources of his resentment. To the extent that the narrative associates Judge Temple's gun, and the hunters' own weapons, with masculine identity, Edwards bears the mark of competition between the patriarch and an overtaking man of the next generation. Though Edwards feels compelled to repress his anger, Natty feels free to voice a sarcastic attack on the true subject of the dispute – Temple's manliness. He speaks scornfully of "that popgun in your hand," and accuses the Judge of taming the game to compensate for his inadequacy as a marksman: "the snowbirds are flying round your own door, where you may feed them with crumbs and shoot them at pleasure any day" (17). To accentuate the underlying deadliness of the debate, Cooper closely links Natty's surliness toward Temple, the verbal equivalent of Edwards's reticence, with the bloody gesture of cutting the deer's throat: " 'Let who will kill him,' said the hunter, rather surlily, 'I suppose the cretur [*sic*] is to be eaten.' So saying, he drew a large knife from a leathern sheath which was stuck through his girdle or sash and cut the throat of the animal" (18). Later, Cooper will repeat the gesture to mark Natty's yielding to the temptation of his own blood lust. Here the sudden shock of the thrust and the attention to the knife, its sheath, and its position in the girdle at his waist associate it with Natty's smoldering anger and the lingering rudeness of his challenge to the Judge's maleness. That throughout the scene the foresters' anger seems out of keeping with the Judge's good humor emphasizes the advantages of Temple's power. To the victim, the impulsive exercise of masculine potency was no laughing matter.

The competition between Temple and Edwards becomes still more sexually charged as Cooper develops the strong, physical attraction between the wounded youth and the Judge's daughter Elizabeth. Because of his interest in male relationships and his scorn for the genteel, even D. H. Lawrence misses the explicit sexuality of their pairing. Cooper goes well beyond the traditional romantic emphasis on Elizabeth's raven locks, although even here the pairing of the hero and heroine adds a narcissistic erotic element – Oliver's "hair rivaled in color and gloss the locks of Elizabeth" (80). The attraction between Elizabeth and the young hunter advances in carefully choreographed stages of disrobing. Edwards moves irresistibly into the sleigh of his enemy after Elizabeth "regardless of the cold air, . . . threw back the hood which concealed her features" (24). Her "gaze" is in turn drawn to him in the hall after he removes his cap to expose the raven locks. She watches as by an "act and attitude that were both involuntary," Edwards betrays the complexity of his feelings for father and daughter in a gesture that we might more readily expect to find in *The Blithedale Romance* than in the Leatherstocking tales:

> The hand [Oliver's] that held the cap rested lightly on the little ivory-mounted piano of Elizabeth, with neither rustic restraint nor obtrusive vulgarity. A single finger touched the instrument, as if accustomed to dwell on such places. His other arm was extended to its utmost length, and the hand grasped the barrel of his long rifle, with something like convulsive energy. (80)

Of course, on a genteel level the double gesture expresses the contrast between the youth's still secret social status and the wildness of his current life. But to leave it at that is to accept too easily that one hand doesn't know what the other is doing. Elizabeth, at least, senses that Oliver's presence unites the convulsive phallic gesture, tense with the unvoiced anger at the patriarch, and the gesture of the single finger that knows how to play Elizabeth's "instrument as if accustomed to dwell in such places"; she continues to gaze at his "wonderfully speaking lineaments" (81). Lost as if in "deep abstraction," Elizabeth watches as he throws aside his overcoat and then starts from the room "colouring excessively" when he pauses before baring his wounded shoulder (94).

Elizabeth has come home to take the place of her dead mother as mistress of her father's house, and the narrative repeatedly emphasizes the emotional closeness of father and daughter. In both the opening forest scene and the account of their entrance into the Judge's house, Cooper calls up the memory of the missing mother. He lingers over the "form of exquisite proportions, rather full and rounded for her years [that Elizabeth] inherited from her mother" (78). In his immediate attraction to Elizabeth, Edwards falls into a competition with strong oedipal overtones. Cooper underscores the competition between the older and younger man by dwelling on Elizabeth's sexuality and by placing her in the generationally ambiguous role of mistress of her father's house.

Though the images of Elizabeth's filial closeness to Judge Temple, on the one hand, and of Edwards's angry competitiveness, on the other, represent contrasting extremes of Cooper's possible relationship to his father's patriarchal authority, they alike implicate a high degree of emotional involvement with the father inconsistent with fully developed maturity and independence. Elizabeth, at eighteen, is close to womanhood – in the world of the novel, only her status as daughter, rather than as wife, prevents full recognition of her maturity. Edwards, on the other hand, though five years older than Elizabeth, seems childishly temperamental to readers and characters alike; his anger traps him in delayed adolescence. In *The Pioneers*, Cooper's evolving narrative stance toward the history of Templeton and its founder represents an increasingly successful effort to negotiate a median way between these suggested extremes – a way that enables Cooper to gain control over his personal past and transform it into fiction.

Through the first fifteen chapters, Cooper controls his material more by his tone than by the plotting of a narrative line. He approaches the discursive survey of frontier life with what might best be classified as celebratory irony. Chief among its virtues, the ironic stance establishes the necessary distance both from the patriarch's power and Oliver Edwards's chokingly obsessive preoccupation with it. By means of ironic good humor, Cooper armed himself against his fears that returning to the story of his youth might demonstrate his subservience to his father. If he treated William Cooper and Cooperstown reverently or even with the straightforward puffing of the Judge's own *A Guide in the Wilderness*, he would confirm his father's preeminence. In later years, when his need to identify with his father and *patria* was as great as his youthful desire to maintain independence had been, he would commit himself to the service of writing *The Chronicles of Cooperstown*, but in 1822 he secured a safe outside perspective from which he could make fun of the Judge's foibles. Though the opening scene dramatizes some of Cooper's deepest ambivalences about his father, he maintains control over the conflicting participants. Judge Temple's liability to error and boastfulness checks the force of his authority; Oliver Edwards's susceptibility to Elizabeth's charms and his fondness for melodramatic gestures casts suspicion on his stoicism; Natty's sense of wrong is qualified by his sulkiness; and even Elizabeth is later chided for occasional hautiness. By establishing distance on his American scene, Cooper creates a stylistic safe haven. He may come forward to celebrate the vitality of father and frontier, but he can always slide back with ease to his vantage point of amused superiority.

Cooper calls particular attention to Elizabeth's "playful voice"; within the narrative her laconic joking sounds the note of Cooper's own vantage point. Asked by her father whether he is "compos mentis or not? – Fit to charge a grand jury, or . . . able to do the honors of a Christmas-eve in the hall of Templeton?" Elizabeth replies from under her hood, "More able to do either, my dear father . . . than to kill deer with a smooth-bore" (41). By picking up on the Leatherstocking's deprecation of her father's shooting without his bitterness, Elizabeth brings the spirit of Natty's silent laugh, expressive "of exultation, mirth, and irony," into the decorum of her affectionate loyalty to her father (28). Because, unlike Natty, she feels unthreatened by his authority, she can play his foibles off against his manly good humor.

Playfulness is an essential part of Cooper's ironic strategy. In Cooper's narrative voice, as in Elizabeth's joking, playfulness implies a degree of confidence that allows Cooper to move closer to his father. Juxtaposed to the idea of irony as a place of retreat, this may seem paradoxical. But Cooper did not propose to gain distance on his father only to knock him down – to tar and feather the kinsman as totem of authority. He meant, rather, to gain sufficient control so that he could approach his father's authority and incorporate it within his own creation and so attain for himself the status of founder.

Maintaining an association between his own irony and Elizabeth's eye for the frontier's comparative roughness, Cooper persistently delimits the claims of Temple's patriarchal ambitions. Following Elizabeth's eye from the broad overview of Templeton to the awkward architecture of Judge Temple's mansion and the houses for which it served as a less-than-Platonic "model" for imitation, the narrator wryly declares that "the occupants of these favored habitations were the nobles of Templeton, as Marmaduke was its king" (50, 46; Nevius, 1– 33). In *A Guide in the Wilderness,* William Cooper defends at great length his policy of severely restricting the size of town lots. His town owed its economic vitality, he believed, to his policy of grouping stores in convenient proximity and limiting the tradesman's temptation to divide his labor by farming. To the narrator of *The Pioneers,* however, the houses "were grouped together in a manner that aped the streets of a city"; looking "to the wants of posterity" had its absurd aspect (45). The father's favored cause becomes, in the son's treatment, a sign of provincial deference "to the condition of the old, or, as they expressed it, the *down* countries; . . . surely nothing could look more like civilization than a city, even if it lay in a wilderness!" (68).

Though the narrator's irony makes its appeal to the superiority of an initiated genteel audience, it keeps one foot in the rough-edged camp of the frontier and never loses its ability to celebrate Templeton's primitive vitality. Even in a scene as potentially ludicrous as Temple's howled greetings to his dogs, Cooper avoids unbridled ridicule:

> There was a general rush from [the] kennel, accompanied with every canine tone, from the howl of the wolf-dog to the petulant bark of the terrier. The master received their boisterous salutations with a variety of imitations from his own throat, when the dogs, probably from shame of being outdone, ceased their outcry. (73)

Temple's obliviousness to genteel propriety – in short, to the point of view of those initiated to the narrative's irony – increases our sense of his manly self-assuredness; we admire him the more as he fails to conform to the "civilized" standards that make possible our ironic distance from him.

Irony, of course, implies a double perspective; Cooper's ability, suggested by the passage above, to credit the naïve as well as the initiated point of view corresponds to one of the most important stylistic advances Cooper achieves in the Leatherstocking tales. Because modern readers look back to Cooper past the achievements of Hawthorne and Melville and through the lens of Mark Twain's satire, they inevitably find it easier to see the distance between Cooper's style and later nineteenth-century achievements than to hear how Cooper, or for that

matter Scott before him, led prose style away from fading eighteenth-century models. But Cooper knew the value of frontier
language even as he pointed out its bombastic puffery. Although
Cooper lampoons the public "resolutions" printed in the "most
conspicuous columns of a little, blue-looking newspaper," he,
nevertheless, exploits the journal's hyperbolic phrases to celebrate the patriarch's ubiquitous optimism and the village's sense
of integration with the democratic experiment at large:

> To these flourishing resolutions, which briefly recounted the
> general utility of education, the political and geographical
> rights of the village of Templeton to a participation in the
> favors of the regents of the university, the salubrity of the air,
> and wholesomeness of the water, together with the cheapness
> of food, and the superior state of morals in the neighborhood,
> were uniformly annexed, in large Roman capitals, the names
> of Marmaduke Temple, as chairman, and Richard Jones, as
> secretary. (124)

Hovering between parody and stylistic homage, Cooper's experimental incorporation of frontier hyperbole resists the tendency of irony to stagnate in a fixed position of superiority.
The balanced enjoyment of his own superiority, on the one
hand, and of his father's frontier energy, on the other, succeeds
in invigorating his own literary style.

The importance of protecting the admirable qualities of the
frontier patriarch while, at the same time, limiting the sense of
his power through an ironic tone is backed up by a second narrative strategy; in essence, Richard Jones, Marmaduke Temple's
cousin and lieutenant in enterprise, serves as a comic double of
the Judge's patriarchal ambitions. They are paired from the outset not only by Richard's insistence on their kinship but also by
the narrator's comment that Richard stands in for Temple as
master of the Negro Agamemnon – "owing to the religious
scruples of the Judge" against slavery – and by the unstated
parallel between the Judge's shooting accident and Richard's life-
threatening sleighing upset, both consequences of vaunts of
prowess (63). Richard's invariable determination, for example,
"to participate in the business at hand, let it be what it would"

and his "zeal for preeminence" allow Cooper an opportunity to poke fun at William Cooper's consuming interest in every aspect of his settlers' lives and his well-known political and physical aggressiveness, but they leave Cooper room to celebrate the community's true respect for his patriarchal concern – on Christmas Eve each man in the tavern comes up to shake Temple's "offered hand" (137, 233, 202). Through Richard, Cooper can ridicule the more extreme tendencies of his father's patriarchal ambition without the anxiety of taking on his father or the risk of too deeply undermining his fictional patriarch's stature.

As a method of negotiating a fictional response to his father's authority, Cooper's irony was insufficient in one crucial respect. It provided no solutions to the problem of plot. With the exception of the first scene, the opening fifteen chapters offer readers almost no plotted action. For all the intellectual superiority of the ironic narrator's perspective, he remains a camp follower to the extent that the narration is "descriptive" rather than comprising a fictional "tale." Although approaching his father's accomplishments ironically allowed Cooper independence from his emotional responses to his father's presence, it dictated a degree of subservience. Although James Cooper controls how we see it, William Cooper dictates what we see.

Cooper felt the discomfort of the contradiction embodied in his classification of *The Pioneers* as "A Descriptive Tale." In chapter eight, he invokes his desire "to establish the fidelity of our narrative," but after a long account of the origins of immigrant populations on the frontier, he apologetically closes the chapter: "After this digression, we shall return to our narrative" (110, 131). In this symptomatic juxtaposition, "fidelity" to the facts of frontier life results in "digression" – in a loss of narrative control. In the particular context, the truthful account of the mixed population supports Templeton's status as a representative town on the New York frontier. But this demographic truth remains a "digression" from the "narrative" until Cooper gains sufficient control over the material to free the facts from "fidelity" and weave them into the dynamic frontier synecdoche he makes of Templeton later in the novel. In a broader sense, he apologizes for the long "descriptive" aspect of the novel because he remains, to an uncomfortable extent, in the service of his father's accomplishment. If readers were to feel the authority of his narrative, Cooper had to achieve more control over the material of his childhood than irony alone allowed.

For Cooper, the problems of excessive description, subservience to his father's history, and stagnating narrative action were all related, and it is not surprising that his experiments to escape these problems were similarly interwoven in the central scenes of *The Pioneers*.

Commanding the center of the novel, a succession of three communal ventures transforms the meandering descriptive tale into a structured and symbolically charged narrative empowered with mythopoetic force. Each scene begins as a public procession out from the patriarch's house into the community – to oversee the maple sugaring, to shoot flocks of passenger pigeons, to seine bass from the lake – and closes by taking note of personal responses to the expeditions as the group turns homeward. By manipulating his narrative point of view with increasing skill, Cooper sets readers in progressively more complex relationships to the unfolding conflicts.

Each of the central scenes is undisguisedly staged; and, after the digressive opening, the note of artifice increases, rather than diminishes, the sense that at long last we are confronting the elemental forces at work on the frontier. On the way to the maple groves, Marmaduke Temple's household moves "through the village in great order," and in the expedition's ceremonial aspect readers sense immediately Cooper's assertion of narrative control. Through a simple yet magnificent simile, Cooper places his line of forest pilgrims in reverential awe of the grove opening before them:

> . . . they reached an open wood on the summit of the moun-
> tain, where the hemlocks and pines totally disappeared, and
> a grove of [maples] covered the earth with their tall, straight
> trunks and spreading branches, in stately pride. The under-
> wood had been entirely removed from this grove . . . and a
> wide space of many acres was cleared, which might be likened
> to the dome of a mighty temple, to which the maples with
> their stems formed the columns, their tops composing the
> capitals, and the heavens the arch. (294)

As if they had entered a cathedral, "silence" falls over their divided "discourse" on business and love (293–94). For a brief moment, passions, so important to each individual, involuntarily shrink to insignificance before their shared awe. In visual terms, Cooper emphasizes the change by pulling back abruptly from his narrow focus on individual conversants, to a broader prospect that dwarfs his characters beneath the natural arches looming above them.

When the very next sentence pulls the reader's eye from lofty contemplation to the "deep and careless incision that had been made into each tree, near its root," we feel the shock of deeply opposed principles. The aesthetic disjunction caused by leaving the curving heavenward ascent along column, capital, and arch to face the bruising gashes of the ax deepens the reader's sense of the violation against nature. By referring to the grove as a "temple," Cooper associates the moment of reverence with the patriarch's protective concern for the trees. The gashes are the work of Billy Kirby.

In this and succeeding central scenes, Kirby elevates the sense of conflict because Cooper, in first characterizing the woodchopper, transcends the limitations of the descriptive mode. To advance the work's demographic accuracy, Cooper had frequently stalled the early chapters of his narrative with the histories of subordinate characters like Doctor Todd, the Reverend Grant, the French storekeeper, the prosperous German farmer, the ex-soldier, and the Yankee lawyer. But in his account of Billy Kirby, Cooper quickly establishes a difference. Kirby's "great stature" marks him as more than a representative woodchopper; his history subsumes the histories of all the others. Armed with an ax and a rifle, he projects the force of the entire westward migration. In the place of particular personal or historical details used to establish other characters, Cooper presses toward the epic: "with the tread of Hercules," Kirby approaches trees "towering apparently into the very clouds" and selects "one of the most noble for the first trial of his power" (248). Where the past tense used in other histories moved readers away from the main narrative line, Cooper's frequent use of present participles and his emphasis on the habitual nature of Kirby's actions – "he would shoulder his ax," "he would strike a light blow"

– bring Kirby's actions into the present. Because of Cooper's remarkable compression, the final, slightly ambiguous allusion to Kirby's place in the history of epic – or is it barbarian? – conquest comes as swiftly as the destruction of the forest:

> . . . his logging ended, with a dispatch that could only ac-
> company his dexterity and Herculean strength, the jobber
> would collect together his implements of labor, light the heaps
> of timber, and march away, under the blaze of the prostrate
> forest, like the conqueror of some city, who, having first pre-
> vailed over his adversary, places the final torch of destruction,
> as the finishing blow to his conquest. (249)

Liberating Kirby from the particular historical record of one frontier town and endowing him with epic resonance liberated William Cooper's son from his documentary role and lifted the Cooperstown frontier beyond its place at a particular moment in the country's and his personal past. With a confidence missing since the first scene of the novel, Cooper gains the narrative leverage to move rather than follow his characters. In the sugaring scene, he sets Kirby in dynamic opposition to Temple and allows him to rebut the Judge's condemnation of Americans' wasteful reaction to abundance:

> "I'm sure the country is in a thriving way; and, though I know
> you calkilate greatly on the trees, setting as much store by
> them as some men would by their children, yet, to my eyes
> they are a sore sight at any time, unless I'm privileged to work
> my will on them; in which case, I can't say but they are more
> to my liking." (301)

The terms of the opposition are fascinating in themselves. Cooper introduced both Judge Temple and Billy Kirby through accounts of their shooting; the language of masculine prowess has already been established as the essential manifestation, if not the determining impulse, of the pioneer's relationship to the natural and social worlds. Under the arching maples, Kirby extends the use of alternative masculine stances in order to define the different responses to the American landscape. The Judge extends his patriarchal responsibility out from his daughter and community to American resources, treating trees as some men would "their children"; Kirby cannot rest till he has forced the forest into supine submission. On the one hand, the language deepens the sense of opposition. The Judge promises nurture and, by implication, extends to nature a familial relationship that taboos it against misuse. Kirby's uninhibited desire – "to work my will on them" – attaches the destructive potential of sexual compulsion and rape to the doctrine of use and man's rightful command over lower orders of creation. Yet the facts that both responses are cast in masculine terms, that we have seen the patriarch himself tempted by the desire to work his will on the charging buck, that Kirby and Temple converse without rancor, and that they are equally voices of American civilization all point to the elusive nature of this seemingly clear and decided opposition (Kolodny 91). We have seen, and in the following two scenes will see again, that the patriarchal impulse can slide into more direct assertions of masculine power. Cooper forces us to acknowledge that patriarchal power, even in its most nurturing forms, may break into a more threatening thrust for domination.

As Cooper draws toward the central scenes, he experiments with his most important stylistic strategy for gaining control over the history of his *patria:* the ability to limit and shift his reader's angle of vision. His experiments with point of view begin as rudimentary attempts to register the power of one character's presence by noting its effect on an observer: "With an air of mingled curiosity and jealousy," the Judge's house-keeper, Remarkable Pettibone, watches Elizabeth Temple throw off her outer garments and sees "her own power" ended by the womanly dignity revealed (77). In a more sustained way, Cooper traces Elizabeth's growing interest in Oliver Edwards, otherwise veiled from her companions by her good-humored irony. By moving us into Elizabeth's perspective, where Louisa Grant cannot follow, Cooper sets the erotic aspect of her attraction in opposition to the meeker interest of her friend. Listening to the howl of a wolf at night, Louisa is afraid; Elizabeth immediately associates the wild cries with the hut of Leatherstocking to which Oliver has just retreated; she exults in the contrast between the luxurious warmth of her bed and the wildness of the distant howls, as she feels excited by the contradictions in Oliver's manners. Others take his Indian background literally; she smiles and welcomes it as a sexually charged allusion.

Generally intended to register the private meaning of public scenes, these relatively simple experiments gained more importance when combined with Cooper's increasing sense of pictorial control. In the account of a Christmas turkey shoot preceding the central scenes, Cooper begins to associate his ability to narrow in on a particular conversation with a painter's ability to compose his canvas and alter his perspective. In order to give more weight to a conversation between the Judge and Oliver Edwards, Cooper directs Richard Jones and his continuing chatter away from center stage: "Richard here took occasion to whisper to the young lady, who had shrunk a little from the foreground of the picture" (263). The significance here lies less in the particular design of the scene than in Cooper's self-conscious acknowledgment of his active role in scenic composition. When his scenes shift from the "descriptive" mode to one more self-consciously composed, the landscape opens to interpretation. Both characters and readers are tested by their ability to read it.

The full power of the sugaring scene waits on the final visual framing of the scene created by Elizabeth Temple's backward glance. After a "consoling reflection" that the law would eventually protect the woods against the popular will, Marmaduke remounted.

> . . . the equestrians passed the sugar-camp on their way to the promised landscape of Richard. The woodchopper was left alone, in the bosom of the forest, to pursue his labours. Elizabeth turned her head, when they reached the point where they were to descend the mountain, and thought that the slow fires, that were glimmering under his enormous kettles, his little brush shelter, covered with pieces of hemlock bark, his gigantic size, as he wielded his ladle with a steady and knowing air, aided by the background of stately trees, with their sprouts and troughs, formed, altogether, no unreal picture of human life in its first stages of civilization. (301–02)

Elizabeth's reading of the final framed landscape invites the reader to move one step further. For her the single image represents the rough strength, energy, and primitiveness of frontier life; but we have witnessed this landscape over time. In our reading, Billy Kirby's debate with the Judge adds a more dynamic sense than Elizabeth has of the governing tensions inherent in the frontier. His physical domination of the visual scene dismisses patriarchal care and gives the last word to aggressive masculine volition. In short, pictorial control, when combined with Cooper's increasing confidence in his ability to maneuver his characters and shape the action, opens the possibility of sustained symbolic action.

The second central scene, depicting the slaughter of passenger pigeons, develops the complexity of Cooper's shifts in point of view. The chapter opens with the narrator's magnificent account of spring's final triumph over winter: in their cumulative strength, the little billows overcome the lingering field of ice on Lake Otsego, dispossessing two eagles from their frozen dominion as surely as the westward migration has overrun Natty and the Mohegan's hunting ground (Beard). Though obviously a fine example of Cooper's increasing imaginative authority, the opening account of spring also establishes a narrative point of view so elevated that readers feel the sudden shift down into the concerns of Temple's household as a fall into an inevitably more limited vision of experience.

The call for pigeon shooting comes from Richard Jones, and initially the narrative perspective looks on the village's bustling preparations as if in acceptance of Richard's "animated appeal" (320); the Judge and Edwards seem "equally to participate" in the sight "exhilarating to a sportsman" (321). But when "the tall, gaunt form of Leather-stocking" moves into the field, the narrative shifts away from Jones and aligns itself with Natty's "feelings at this wastefull and unsportsmanlike execution" (322). While all the village looks upward to the flock, Cooper turns the reader's eyes downward; like Natty, each reader becomes "a silent, but uneasy spectator" of the game "none pretended to collect" lying "scattered over the fields in such profusion as to cover the very ground with fluttering victims" (324).

After Natty shoots his single bird, Marmaduke Temple begins to sense his proper alliance with Natty's condemnation of "wasty ways" – ways that blur, as did Kirby's crude incisions, the line between use and destruction. But when Natty leaves, looking down to pick his way among the wounded birds, Marmaduke again looks upward, tempted by the next flock "in common with the rest," and brings "his musket to his shoulder" (328). Only after the superfluous destruction caused by the cannon shot does Temple succeed in keeping his eye in line with the narrator's and Leatherstocking's. When Richard Jones proclaims "Victory," Marmaduke answers, "Not so, Dickon, . . . the field is covered with them; and, like the Leather-stocking, I see nothing but eyes, in every direction, as the innocent sufferers turn their heads, in terror, to examine my movements. Full one half of those that have fallen are yet alive: and I think it is time to end the sport; if sport it be" (329).

The shifts in angle of vision take the symbolic power achieved by pictorial framing and push it into action. As Cooper alters his narrative perspective, readers witness the difficulty of transferring Natty's way of seeing nature to democratic society en masse. Because readers gain access to the scene of slaughter through competing perspectives, they cannot remain aloof as they could more easily earlier in the narrative. Instead, they participate in Richard's excitement, in Natty's watchful disgust, in Temple's struggle between the view along his gun barrel and the sight of broken innocents at his feet. Finally, Temple, though affected himself, leaves the field, despairing of achieving more control over the slaughter than he can by the compromise of sending children out to wring the necks of the wounded birds. The reader is left to watch the horses "loaded with the dead" and to take note of Richard Jones and Ben Pump, whose views are unchanged (330).

Set on a cloud-darkened evening, Cooper's evocation of night fishing by a bonfire's uneven light marks the definitive success of his effort to transmute the memories of his childhood into the malleable materials of his art. Assembling the Judge's householders, the villagers, and finally the foresters of Natty's cabin in a single circle of light, the scene achieves a rough grandeur, as if a dark Wagnerian chorus curled its march around the fire of a peasant folktale. As Cooper presses the new lessons of his craft, shifting narrative perspective more often and boldly exploiting the chiaroscuro of his canvas, he draws readers further into the scene. No longer ironic onlookers, viewing the action from a safe distance, readers find themselves in a new and uncertain relation to the scene and to its narrator.

From the start, Cooper calls attention to the importance of perspective. Accompanied by his daughter, Louisa Grant, and Oliver Edwards, Marmaduke Temple chooses to walk to the fishing grounds along the lakeside where, from "high grassy banks," they watch the fishermen in their boat "moving with great rapidity across the lake, until it entered the shade of the western hills, and was lost to the eye" (333). Even when they approach more closely, Marmaduke urges them to maintain their chosen high ground in order to "examine" the fishing party "below them" (334). From this distance, the fishermen become "figures moving around the light," and as "figures" they comprise, in Elizabeth's view, a "picture" open to interpretation (334, 347). She reads the glimmering flame as an emblem of her impatient cousin Richard Jones: "and see; it begins to fade again, like most of his brilliant schemes" (334). Jocular though she is, we too hear her command to "see," and to our eyes both the figures around the fire and those figures watching from the bank become the subjects of Cooper's portfolio. Over the next two chapters, Cooper displays his sketches – a deliberate series, all of the same dark scene, but from different points of vision.

Uniting the series is the rich play of light and dark. From the high perspective of the bank, Cooper zooms in "so near to the flame" that he can trace the smoke sliding across Ben Pump's face (334). In both the long and short views, he stresses the limits of vision: "The stars were obscured by the clouds . . . the smoke occasionally obscured his solemn visage" (334). In fact, darkness not only frames each picture, it also accounts for the distinctiveness of individual perspectives. In the wide horizon of daylight, small variations in position make little difference in what the eye takes in, but in the moral night hanging over Cooper's villagers, small displacements signify: each person in the party of "turbulent passions" is ringed by his or her own darkness (338).

Under Cooper's hand, the chiaroscuro underscores both the essential importance and the extraordinary difficulty of *seeing* –

of seeing what Yvor Winters would have claimed as the rich "moral substance" implicit in the scene (186). In the deprivation of such darkness, each illuminated gesture gains significance. Since, for example, we are offered only a momentary view of Billy Kirby "standing with his feet in the water, at an angle of forty-five degrees, inclining shorewards, and expending his gigantic strength," that "posture," like the attitude of candlelit figures in a de La Tour, speaks to us synecdochically (340–41). In Kirby's inclination, Cooper draws the unthinking and concentrated passion of the entire village.

On the other hand, Cooper repeatedly focuses on the nearly impenetrable darkness. His description of the view from the fireside out over the lake illustrates the essence of Cooper's visual strategy throughout the night scene. Though it presents itself as a landscape, it achieves its beauty and uncanny power as much by obscuring the reader's sight as by opening a prospect. The more readers look, the more they are closed in:

> The night had now become so dark as to render objects, without the reach of the light from their fire, not only indistinct, but, in most cases, invisible. For a little distance the water was discernible, glistening, as the glare from the fire danced over its surface, touching it, here and there, with red quivering streaks; but at a hundred feet from the shore, a boundary of impenetrable gloom opposed itself to the vision. One or two stars were shining through the openings of the clouds, and the lights were seen in the village, glimmering faintly, as if at an immeasurable distance. At times, as their fire lowered, or as the horizon cleared, the outline of the mountain, on the other side of the lake, might be traced, by its undulations; but its shadow was cast, wide and dense, on the bosom of the waters, rendering the darkness, in that direction, trebly deep. (338)

Under the pressure of Cooper's repeated attention, the "obscurity" of the night takes on the quality of metaphor and "like the gloom of oblivion, [seems] to envelope the rest of the creation" (346). It becomes not only the encircling void waiting for short lives to flicker and fade like brands from the fire, but the enveloping medium of the characters' lives. And in this case, the obscurity of the medium is Cooper's message. Again and again during the two-chapter scene, Cooper notes the difficulty of seeing. Watching boats disappear into the darkness or flash "into the circle of light," Elizabeth "strained her eyes" to see (340, 341).

As if in acknowledgment of the narrative power he gained by narrowing his readers' vision, Cooper stresses a second obstacle to seeing clearly. The difficulty can be defined in terms of the ability of the noun "sight" to signify both the faculty of vision and the object perceived. In this scene, "sights" of the objective kind actively assert their power over the characters who behold them. When Elizabeth strains to look through the darkness, she experiences difficulty as an active subject in search of an elusive object, but at several points in the chapter, Cooper uses the passive voice to suggest that people may act impulsively – without a clear vision of their own actions – because the "sight" they see acts more powerfully on their passions than the power of their insight can act to decipher the picture before them.

Cooper first introduces the idea of the viewer's passivity before the "sight" in a relatively neutral way – by noting that "the appearance of the fire urged the pedestrians on, for even the ladies had become eager to witness the miraculous draught" (334). But at a crucial moment, when Temple and Edwards complete their descent from the aloof perspective of the grassy bank to full participation in the village's prodigality, Cooper reverts to the passive voice: "Yielding to the excitement of the moment," Temple lays his hands to the net beside Billy Kirby, who has been "inflamed beyond the bounds of discretion at the sight" (342). Edwards had preceded Temple, Cooper observes, "for the sight of the immense piles of fish, that were slowly rolling over on the gravelly beach, had impelled him also to leave the ladies, and join the fishermen" (248). Instead of penetrating the darkness, sight draws the seer into the night's "turbulent passions."

After Oliver Edwards and Temple have joined the fish seining, Cooper pulls back from the commotion at lakeside to frame the action and bring it into interpretable order. He creates a distance from the objects and thus frees readers to use their sight rather than be overcome by the "sight" that they see. Once again

Cooper uses Elizabeth's backward glance to establish the narrative perspective and makes the importance of visual composition even more explicit:

> Elizabeth and her friend strolled to a short distance from the group, along the shores of the lake. After reaching a point, to which even the brightest of the occasional gleams of light from the fire did not extend, the ladies turned, and paused a moment, in contemplation of the busy and lively party they had left. . . .
>
> "This is indeed a subject for the pencil!" exclaimed Elizabeth. "Observe the countenance of the woodchopper, while he exults in presenting a larger fish than common to my cousin Sheriff; and see, Louisa, how handsome and considerate my dear father looks, by the light of that fire, where he stands viewing the havoc of the game. He seems really melancholy, as if he actually thought that a day of retribution was to follow this hour of abundance and prodigality! Would they not make a fine picture, Louisa?" (346–47)

For Cooper, these paragraphs enact a major achievement: in a departure from the earlier study of the maple grove, this "picture" includes Judge Temple within the aesthetic boundaries of Elizabeth's glance. The scene itself embodies Cooper's larger achievement: he transforms Judge Cooper into a "figure" within the frame of his narrative. Instead of dominating his youngest son, the father has become a fictional character the son can place in opposition to Billy Kirby or Natty Bumppo as another representative of continuing forces on the frontier. The parallel phrases, opening and closing the paragraph – "This is indeed a subject for the pencil!"; "Would they not make a fine picture, Louisa?" – insist on the control of artistic vision. However large the model in real life, inside the enclosing frame of art the "original" father will be kept to the scale of the canvas and placed in the service of the artist's claim to originality.

As if exhilarated by the triumph of bringing his father under artistic control, Cooper presses his advantage to secure authority over his readers. In this self-reflexive passage, Cooper holds back from the neat, almost allegorical reading of the "picture" offered at the end of the sugaring scene, when Elizabeth thought that Billy Kirby's encampment "formed, altogether, no unreal picture of human life in its first stages of civilization" (302). For, as readers have learned moving through the fishermen's flickering light, Cooper's pictorial mode moves us into the darkness and fosters experience less easily read than the neat formulation Elizabeth seeks. The deepest experiences encouraged by Cooper's chiaroscuro and his control of perspective are these sensations of straining through darkness, of turning to objects suddenly and momentarily illuminated: of seeking the firelight as if we ourselves were the uneasy victims of the seine. Such experiences resist formulaic interpretation; they lead instead to deeper participation in the impulses of characters moved by private and communal passions unsorted and unnamed.

Although Cooper allows Elizabeth's empathetic reading of her father's mood to pass unquestioned, he takes her to task for her teasing attempt to push Louisa Grant toward a facile reading of the scene. Elizabeth acts as if responses to visual composition were a sort of parlor game. As Elizabeth guesses, Louisa has fallen in love with Oliver Edwards, and the minister's daughter stumbles painfully when she tries to shield her emotional connection to the scene:

> "Well, then, if I may venture an opinion," said Louisa, timidly, "I should think it might indeed make a picture. The selfish earnestness of that Kirby over his fish would contrast finely with the – the – expression of Mr. Edwards's face. I hardly know what to call it; but it is – a – is – you know what I would say, dear Elizabeth."
>
> "You do me too much credit, Miss Grant," said the heiress; "I am no diviner of thoughts, or interpreter of expressions."
>
> There was certainly nothing harsh, or even cold, in the manner of the speaker, but still it repressed the conversation. (347)

The edge of nastiness in Elizabeth Temple's response is not excused by the possible recognition of her "improper phraseology" (347). Despite her claims to the contrary, Elizabeth understands Louisa's feelings perfectly, and for a woman who somewhat imperiously asked her friend to "Call me by my Christian name" in the preceding line, Elizabeth's "Miss Grant" is both harsh and cold, especially as a response to Louisa's "dear

Elizabeth." Her tone marks her own competing interest in Oliver Edwards. Elizabeth is an "heiress," and, like her father, she lets her power speak.

Their conflict springs to the surface because of Elizabeth's misguided and inadequate notion of interpretation. Louisa's nakedly intimate reading is too personal to include the tensions woven into the scene during the previous chapter. Yet even purely personal responses are too emotionally complex to fit neat, epigrammatic interpretations. Louisa's language cannot bridge the gap between private and public; Elizabeth's effort to deny altogether her role as an "interpreter of expressions" is a similar, and hardly more adroit, effort to deny the scene's emotional meaning for her. For these characters, as for the reader, the "picture" operates on an emotional level resistant to simple readings.

Cooper's placement of this interchange in the larger structure of the scene enforces his critique of such incomplete readings. Elizabeth's retreat from the fishermen clearly parallels the Judge's earlier decision to pause on the high bank before descending to the shore; together the two overviews appear to frame the scene. But unlike her final survey over Billy Kirby's encampment, Elizabeth's reading is no longer the last word. Instead of coming at the end of the episode, it opens a second chapter deepening the resonance of the fish seining still further and making still more apparent the incompleteness of any summary response.

Cooper breaks the chill silence resulting from Elizabeth's rebuke by turning her "gaze" to the wondrous vision of Natty's canoe coming across the water. She watches the extraordinary passage of Natty's light from "under the brow of the mountain . . . across, or rather over, the lake" where, with its reflection, it forms "an appearance not unlike an inverted note of admiration" (348, 350). Making no further effort to interpret or to shield herself by irony, Elizabeth responds with a simple exclamation: "It is beautiful!" (350). At this point, Cooper has mastered the symbolic possibilities of strong visual composition, and within the scene Elizabeth's words register the kind of aesthetic response that strikes deeper than a formulaic reading. Such wonderfully observed details as the inverted exclamation mark made by Natty's small fire and its watery shadow encourages

readers to look further into the scene and to articulate the oppositions clarified by the contrast of Natty's small still light and
the red glow of the villagers' larger and more uncertain fire
(Dekker 48–49). But those oppositions move us because, like
Elizabeth, we first experience them aesthetically and emotionally
without the distancing mediation of the narrator's interpretation.

After the extraordinary events witnessed by Elizabeth in a
"trance created by this scene" – the gliding hunt of the salmon
trout, the drowning and resurrection of Ben Pump – Cooper
closes the bizarre night revels by framing the scene once more
(358). He returns to Elizabeth's perspective as if he were glossing
both her deepening comprehension and the increasing power of
his visual control. This time the scene is "rendered" but not
read:

> The wood chopper was seen broiling his supper on the coals,
> as [Elizabeth and her father's party] lost sight of the fire; and
> when [their] boat approached the shore, the torch of Mohe-
> gan's canoe was shining again under the gloom of the eastern
> mountain. Its motion ceased suddenly; a scattering of brands
> was exhibited in the air, and then all remained dark as the
> conjunction of night, forests, and mountains could render the
> scene.
>
> The thoughts of the heiress wandered from [Edwards], who
> was holding a canopy of shawls over herself and Louisa, to
> the hunter and the Indian warrior; and she felt an awakening
> curiosity to visit a hut, where men of such different habits
> and temperament were drawn together, as if by one common
> impulse. (364)

In this, the scene's true ending, Elizabeth returns to the level of
feeling she tried to suppress earlier. She makes no comment,
and even her "thoughts," as the progression of the final paragraph makes clear, can more truly be understood in terms of
her "felt" response to three foresters and the common "impulse"
drawing them together. Over the interpretive power of the
subject's sight, Cooper's closing moment places the power of
the "sight" to move the subject.

Supremely confident in the power of perspective and composition, Cooper leaves his readers with an image as expressive
as it is unexplained. Like Elizabeth's earlier exclamation, our

response is simple and aesthetic: "It is beautiful!" Yet, as Cooper unobtrusively circles back to one more closing picture of Billy Kirby, to the villagers, and to Natty's brand, that aesthetic response seals a final thematic reprise. Nothing could signal more effectively the confident certainty of the pioneers' westward progress than the unemphatic casualness of Billy Kirby's posture as he "stretched his large frame on the grass" to watch his dinner broil on the coals (363). As if in response, Natty's brand, already established as the mark of his stature, is extinguished and he retreats into the darkness. Yet his path is not entirely lost. In a narrative transformation – one that enacts the power of visual images on the beholder's psyche – the brand that dies in the penultimate paragraph becomes the impulse felt by Elizabeth Temple in the last.

Judge Temple's important but restricted role in the closing moments of the scene reveals the correspondence between Cooper's narrative mastery and his efforts to come to terms with his father's achievement. After Natty's rescue of the drowning steward, Judge Temple steps into the chaotic village crowd to assume "direction of matters, with . . . dignity and discretion" (363). And there Cooper leaves him. Insofar as Temple serves as a fictional surrogate of William Cooper, James Cooper acknowledges his father's natural, though hardly omnipotent, command. That was his father's sphere. When the scene shifts to Elizabeth's last gaze, comprehending Kirby's strength and Natty's fading light, the father cannot follow. Judge Temple came as far as recognizing the destructiveness of Kirby's methods, but only his offspring feels a deep, almost involuntary empathy with Natty's life, feels the sadness of his disappearance, and senses the overwhelming power and confidence of Billy Kirby that allies him with the Judge and makes their united conquest inevitable. William Cooper envisioned a settlement in the wilderness; James Cooper, with deeper insight, saw a complex vision of gains and losses and projected it into art.

When Elizabeth Temple's eye rests at last on Natty Bumppo rather than on her own father, she charts Cooper's departure from dependence. He leaves the patriarch by the shore without hostility or vindictiveness. Oliver Edwards, ordinarily the bearer of hostility toward the father, assumes a background role in service to Elizabeth's affectionate impulses. Without belittling his father's achievement, he simply finds release from it. If, in these closing moments, Elizabeth takes on the role of Cooper's muse, her move away from Judge Temple toward Natty is a move away from one father to another – from Cooper's natural father to a father his art had created (Railton 94). Yet she casts her eye toward Natty as she returns to her father's house. Because *The Pioneers* initiates the Leatherstocking tales, most critics have focused on Cooper's alignment with Natty Bumppo. But Cooper wanted not only to rebel against his father's power, but to claim it. It is as founder of the Leatherstocking tales *and* of the series of narratives chronicling the exploits of the American Abraham that Cooper had fathered a new identity.

As Cooper's command of narrative perspective and visual composition became more assured, he became increasingly confident as well about shaping the larger structure of the novel and allowing it to speak for him. Resonant as it is on its own terms, the fish-seining scene strikes deeper undertones in the context of the other central scenes. On the most straightforward level, there is the power of repetition and accumulation. In the scene at Kirby's sugar camp, for example, the country's extravagant waste – in the form of the woodchopper's "dreadful wounds" – takes its toll on American nature alone. In the second scene, however, Cooper's unwavering references to the wounded passenger pigeons as "victims" and his anthropomorphic focus on the mute appeal of their eyes prepares the ground for a more complex reading. By the time he refers to the netted fish as "alarmed victims" struggling "in fruitless efforts for freedom" the thrashing multitude warns of a more troubling sense of waste – a waste that stretches beyond environmental loss to foretell fundamental losses of political opportunity and identity – losses of freedom (342).

Though dictating the progressive momentum of the book's center, the three environmental scenes take their place in a more complete contrapuntal organization. Though relatively complex, the lines of Cooper's structure are clear and strongly felt by the reader. The three public scenes of present temptation and waste interweave with narratives related by Judge Temple and Natty that offer alternative founding legends. After the sugaring scene (chapter 20), Judge Temple recounts the settlement of the village and the wilderness hardships endured by the early pioneers (21); after the narrative proceeds to the pigeon shoot (22) and the fish seining (23 and 24), Cooper raises the issue of Temple's legitimacy by releasing the veiled news of Mr. Effingham's death (25). Next, Natty's recollection of a mountain sanctuary (26), where he felt sheltered as if by a mother and father, asserts the Leatherstocking's counterclaim as the wilderness's natural authority. As the Judge's authority appears to be qualified by his entanglement with the Effinghams, so the final chapter in the central section (27) places Natty's claim in the context of killing the buck out of season. He falls into temptation as did the Judge when he joined in the slaughter of feathery innocents and leaned his weight against the fish seine.

These parallel alternations set the villagers' waste during the fish seining in juxtaposition to the rescue of the first settlers during the "starving time." As Judge Temple narrates the miraculous appearance of herring in Lake Otsego, it seems almost a divine confirmation of the patriarch's claim to authority and fealty:

> "I had hundreds, at that dreadful time, daily looking up to me for bread. The sufferings of their families, and the gloomy prospect before them, had paralyzed the enterprise and efforts of my settlers; hunger drove them to the woods for food, but despair sent them at night, enfeebled and wan, to a sleepless pillow. It was not a moment for inaction. I purchased cargoes of wheat from the granaries of Pennsylvania . . . it was transported on pack-horses into the wilderness, and distributed among my people. Seines were made, and the lakes and rivers were dragged for fish. Something of a miracle was wrought in our favour, for enormous shoals of herring were discovered to have wandered five hundred miles, through the windings of the impetuous Susquehanna, and the lake was alive with their numbers. These were at length caught, and dealt out to the people, with proper portions of salt; and from that moment we again began to prosper." (307–08)

Judge Temple recalls this rescue when he chides Richard Jones and his plans for seining in language that turns the Christian miracle of the loaves and fishes on its head: "Ah! Dickon," cried

Marmaduke, "I have known thee to leave fragments enough behind thee, when thou hast headed a night-party on the lake, to feed a half-dozen famishing families" (232). By picking up on the earlier founding legend, Temple's remarks cast a shadow over the event and raise the specter of deeper self-destructiveness by which Americans in their carelessness unthinkingly destroy the foundation of their promised land (248). What degree of governance can even a deserving authority wield when a society's memory fails to span five short years?

Although it might seem paradoxical, the further Cooper develops his methods of narrative control over the material of Judge Cooper's life, the greater stature Judge Temple achieves as a character. Confident that the narrative structure of these chapters will balance the Judge's claims against his weaknesses and against Natty's counterclaims to "original" status, Cooper allows Judge Temple to speak in his own voice for extended passages and make his case without the interference of an ironic commentary. Furthermore, bringing his father's life under narrative control liberates the full synecdochic power of the frontier patriarch's history. William Cooper delighted in recognizing his own representative status. In *A Guide in the Wilderness,* he offers himself as a model to the many land developers up and down the frontier. But William Cooper represented a class of men and a moment of history; in his founding of Templeton, Judge Temple initiates a paradigmatic clashing of cultural forces that determined and would continue to determine the values of the nation's emerging culture.

The shift away from irony placed Cooper in a more authoritative relationship to his readers as well. In ironic narration, writer and readers are alike members of the superior audience of cognoscenti. Although there is an implicit control in this – the reader must accede to the terms of the writer's superiority or risk slipping into the excluded lower audience – writer and reader share a collegial aloofness from the narrated events. Cooper's descriptive account in the opening fifteen chapters allows readers to see the frontier world in sharp detail, but as long as Cooper's initial tone persists, readers can move back to view the issues of the narrative from the safety and comfort of genteel irony. But as Cooper enforces his control by placing readers within the chiaroscuro scene, determining their perspective, framing the limits of their vision, and more consciously structuring their progress through an organized series of experiences, he claims a more exclusive superiority. Readers join the characters, involved in experiences that strain sight and insight; Cooper remains aloof, an authorial presence who determines, no longer at the behest of his father, how to present the history of the frontier.

4

The Prairie and the Family of an Ishmael

Is it a small thing that thou hast brought us up out of a land that floweth with milk and honey, to kill us in the wilderness, except thou make thyself altogether a prince over us?

Numbers 16:13

In *The Pilot,* Cooper's heroine articulates the patriarchal theory of social development in terms so succinctly typical of seventeenth- and eighteenth-century debates on the role of government that the phrases might have been taken from Filmer's *Patriarcha:* "Are not the relations of domestic life of God's establishing," she asks rhetorically, "and have not nations grown from families, as branches spread from the stem" (192). Like his revolutionary predecessors, Cooper adopts the conservative terms of monarchical justification in order to turn them around and tax the English with their failure to meet the standards of paternal responsibility. But beyond the particular debate within his novels of the Revolution, the assumption of an organic connection between family and society lies at the center of his historical art.

In *The Prairie,* Cooper strips down the social aspects of that central metaphor in order to isolate the family itself as the subject of his inquiry. Both sides of the revolutionary debate relied on the bonds between family members, whether these bonds were described as hierarchical or affectionate, as essential cohesive forces in society. In *The Prairie,* Cooper challenges those assumptions. Instead of using familial metaphors to examine possible social organizations, he examines the nature of the clan itself and argues that its cohesiveness is a product of deadly conflict and struggle. The social achievement presented to the world is not illusory; the clan unites against external forces. But that union is achieved not by inherent familial affection but by the precarious balancing of violently opposed competitors. Writing *The Prairie,* Cooper found it more appropriate to use the vocabulary of revolution and power to describe the family than to rely on factitious models of familial affection and respect to describe society.

Cooper's preoccupation with the threat of patriarchal violence had been paramount as early as *The Spy,* but in that early work he had labored to suppress his apprehensions. His concern that even the most benevolent patriarchal authority might break out in an explosive and arbitrary misuse of power was shared by his countrymen. In *The Spy,* Cooper addressed the nation's continuing uneasiness over the sole stain on George Washington's conduct during the War of Independence: having captured Major André, the British officer who orchestrated Benedict Arnold's betrayal, Washington condemned him to death by hanging. Despite André's reputation for kindness to American prisoners in British hands, Washington refused even his claim as an officer to be executed by firing squad. Fifty years after the Revolution, Washington's life had been apotheosized as the emblem of the country's genesis and the enduring values of the American Republic, yet the success of *The Spy* suggests that readers still sought ways to reconcile those principles to a demonstration of authority so severe, even harsh, that it seemed less in keeping with Washington and the country's image of itself than with the autocratic monarchy the Revolution's rhetoric had so steadily assailed.[1]

To persuade readers that vindictive outbursts were not inherent in the exercise of patriarchal and, consequently, national authority, Cooper's tale distinguishes between Washington's public and private selves. In his public capacity as leader of the American Revolution, Washington remains aloof from the particular actions and characters of the romance – his influence enters the narrative through his order to hang the heroine's Tory brother as an English spy. Yet in his disguise as the private

citizen Mr. Harper, Washington adopts the sons and daughters
of the romance and actively intervenes to rescue the man condemned by his own order. By proposing a double persona for
Washington, Cooper argues that Washington's public role as
father of his country required the sacrifice of a "fallen" son –
that the nation's security created a higher imperative analogous
to God's call to Abraham. The apparent harshness of his judgment against Wharton, Cooper's surrogate for André, should
be understood as an act of parental benevolence to the country
as a whole. On the other hand, Mr. Harper's efforts to release
Wharton offered reassuring evidence of a compassionate private
self searching for ways to stay the commanded sacrifice of Isaac.
The disguise opens up Washington's private motives to inspection and thus counters any suspicions that the harsh public
judgment might itself mask lower motives.

Though persuasive within the terms of *The Spy*, the very
intricacy of the doubling strategy suggests how difficult it was
for Cooper to set aside his sense of explosive patriarchal power.
In *The Prairie*'s pairing of Ishmael Bush and his brother-in-law
Abiram White, the doubling strategy returns to expose the filicidal threat that the earlier romance had sought to suppress.

In all of Cooper's frontier narratives, the relative isolation of
the cast of characters creates a sense of laboratory-like social
experimentation, but this is especially true on the barren plains
of *The Prairie*. Cooper's radical choice of setting measures his
confidence not only by the shift away from the more familiar
forests of the East but also by contrast with the prevailing doubts
of American artists. Bryant's Atheneum Lectures of 1825, although intended to argue against the critical cliché that America
was too new a country to support indigenous writers of romance, have come to serve as touchstones of American anxiety.
It is hard to imagine how an American romancer would have
managed a preface without falling back on the reliable apology
for the inadequacies of the American scene: no history, no society, no manners, no ruins, no romance. On occasion, Cooper
succumbed to this temptation, though one senses a refreshing
self-mockery in his complaint missing from his New England
brethren. It no doubt abetted his complacency that his lament
for the absence of "obscure legends" and "artificial distinctions"

in American history appeared in his preface to the *third* edition of his experimental American work:

> In the *dark ages* of our history, it is true that we hung a few unfortunate women for witches, and suffered some inroads from the Indians; but the active curiosity of the people has transmitted those events with so much accuracy, that there is no opportunity for digression. Then again, notwithstanding that a murder is at all times a serious business, it is much more interesting in a castle than in a corn field. (*The Spy* 7)

In his preface to *The Prairie,* he pays even more cursory homage to the absence of history. He raises the possible objection of a "higher class of readers" to his "selection of a comparative desert, which is aided by no historical recollections, and embellished by few or no poetical associations, for the scene of a legend," only to dismiss it with light-hearted peremptoriness (ix). His earlier successes and recent research into the life of the western tribes assured him that the American landscape offered no insurmountable obstacle to romance. On the contrary, America's vast emptiness was precisely the setting he wanted for this particular inquiry into the most basic human connections.

The power of Cooper's setting depends on its nearly abstract blankness. The family of Ishmael Bush encounters Natty Bumppo at the rim of the world, in a place "bleak and solitary," "remote and unprotected," where the human eye "became fatigued with the sameness and chilling dreariness of the landscape" (16, 19). When Ishmael asks Natty to name the district where they meet, the old trapper points "significantly upward" and asks, "By what name would you call the spot, where you see yonder cloud?" (24). In Cooper's hands, the prairie projects man's existential condition—an insignificant dot in space, living on a "hungry prairie," in a world "no better than a desert" (24, 118). Without Poe's compulsive anxiety, Cooper's landscape projects an image of human ineffectuality and rootlessness of the kind that constantly drives A. Gordon Pym to take his bearings in a desperate effort to feel at home on a blank sea. In those parts of the narrative dominated by Ishmael and his tribe, Cooper maintains an almost Beckett-like abstraction, moving his characters in hopeless circles around the obviously artificial elevation supporting the patriarch's camp and leaving them at last like Vladimir and Estragon under the "ragged and fantastic branches" of a tree whose "white and hoary trunk stood naked and tempest-riven" (486–87).

In *The Prairie,* as in the entire series of romances of frontier settlement, Cooper moves quickly to establish Ishmael's migration as a patriarchal venture: "Thousands of elders . . . were to be seen leading long files of descendants" across the "father of rivers," following the example of the "adventurous and venerable patriarch" of Kentucky (14).[2] Leaving Daniel Boone unnamed, Cooper allows the popular hero's stature, established in countless popular retellings of his story, to extend to his own archetypal pioneer.[3] Yet, uniquely in Cooper's treatment of the frontier patriarch, *The Prairie* never arrives at that transitional stage of development that became Cooper's usual fictional testing ground for social and political issues. Missing from *The Prairie* are extended accounts of a settlement's gradual evolution, of clearing land, building systems of defense, dividing property, establishing trade, and of eventual absorption into the colony or nation. If, in most of his narratives of frontier settlement, Cooper might be said to study the molecular level of society in order to understand the larger national organism, in *The Prairie* he moves inward to examine the forces within the nucleus of the family. Like early atomic scientists, he argued that the entity taken as the basic, stable unit of society could more accurately be described as a potentially explosive union of powerful counterforces. No model of social cohesiveness on the larger molecular scale could afford to ignore the forces that actually comprised the family bond.

This is not to deny Cooper's interest in the annexation of the Louisiana Purchase or in the small European population along the southern Mississippi, decidedly alien in their aristocratic and Catholic sensibilities, but rather to define the romance's particular approach to larger political issues (Porte 50; McWilliams 259). If Cooper had seen the integration of Protestant and Catholic cultures as primary, he might better have set his romance in the New Orleans of 1803, as George Washington Cable did in *The Grandissimes* (1880). Instead, as Joel Porte describes in his reading of the Inez-Middleton romance, Cooper subordinates the cultural question to his more basic study of paternal authority: Cooper moves Inez to the prairie so that "the young American hero [can] be subject to the fructifying influence of Inez's Catholicism without his being forced to accept (indeed, imitate) the Old World father, a symbol of that repressive authority which Protestant America was originally founded to escape" (Porte 50). Cooper's preference for the primitive setting of the plains follows his plan to approach larger social issues through an almost anthropological investigation into the origins of society.

William Wasserstrom first noted how Cooper shared Freud's interest in "reconstructing those events which underlay the creation of social order" and his assumption that events in a "remote time in the history of man" might be reenacted or at least represented by tensions within any familial group (424). Cooper's sense of the cyclical reenactment of history within present stages of development had been sharpened, of course, by his focus on the frontier. Crèvecoeur and Jefferson had given popular expression to *The Prairie*'s underlying assumption that "the gradations of society, from that state which is called refined to that which approaches as near barbarity as connexion with an intelligent people will readily allow, are to be traced from the bosom of the states . . . to those distant, and ever-receding borders" (88). In his constant reliance on the Bible as a source of narrative analogies for the encounters of alien tribes in America, Cooper shared with Freud what remained an essential nineteenth-century anthropological text and created a plot remarkably parallel to the plot of social origins described by Freud:

> The strong male was the master and father of the whole horde, unlimited in his power which he used brutally. All the females were his property, the wives and daughters of his own horde as well as perhaps those stolen from other hordes. The fate of the sons was a hard one; if they excited the father's jealousy they were killed or castrated or driven out. (Wasserstrom 431–32; *Moses and Monotheism* 102–03)

Yet where Freud's general plot reduces countless histories and legends to a common simplicity, Cooper's particular tale elab-

orates it with nearly baroque embellishment – with unlikely
convocations of characters in unlikely places discussing unlikely
themes at unlikely times. *The Prairie* invites readers of Mark
Twain's persuasion to go mad. But as Jane Tomkins notes in
her narrative of literary conversion to an appreciation of Cooper,
it makes little sense to make an aesthetic apology for bizarre
and intricate abstractions when those abstract elements of the
design are essential to the tale's meaning: Cooper's "characters
are elements of thought, things to think with, and the convo-
lutions of the plots, the captures, rescues, and pursuits of the
narrative, are stages in the thought process, phases in a meditation on the bases of social life" (41).

In *The Prairie,* Cooper's meditation turns to the competing
codes and cultures represented by the tale's disparate cast; as
that meditation progresses, the romance comes back repeatedly
to the latent violence within familial bonds and the implications
of that threat on filial obligations. The connections between
segments of the plot and groups of characters – between Ishmael's migration, Natty's solitary life, the kidnapping of Inez,
the presence of a hallucinatory natural scientist, Indian wars,
and more – are indeed convoluted. Cooper deliberately twists
the elements of his tale together – as he spins characters in circles
around the prairie – in order to elaborate on his central issues.
Though the early chapters develop more steadily than later sections of the tale, the nocturnal encounter between Natty and
Ellen Wade noticeably disrupts the pacing of the tale and ex-
emplifies how Cooper uses apparent breaks in the narrative to
establish those issues implicated in the larger actions of the romance.

Stumbling onto a secret rendezvous between Ellen Wade and
the bee hunter, Paul Hover, Natty Bumppo engages the couple
in a lengthy discussion that continues even after the trio's captivity by a band of Sioux attacking Ishmael's camp. The bizarrely
placed conversations divert the reader's perspective from its expected place with either the attackers or their victims. These
interludes violate any number of Mark Twain's rules governing
literary art. By his standards, the episodes have no rightful place
in the work – the characters have only the feeblest excuse for
being where they are, and the conversation seems neither to fit

the given circumstances nor to stop when the people can think of nothing more to say. Yet Cooper's choices are deliberate. Wayne Franklin astutely attributes the woodenness of Cooper's dialogue in the early novels to his "perennial distrust of the social occasion as a moment of truth" (25). By the time of *The Prairie*, the dialogue is no more realistic, but neither is it precisely wooden. Cooper exploits the quirky disjunction of any "social occasion" in a setting so far outside the ken of the novel of manners. He plays on the inappropriateness of lengthy dialogues and quibbles during crucial moments, but he uses the loquacious digressions to articulate the terms of conflicts later staged in the climactic actions of the main narrative with a primal grandeur requiring restraint and silence. Natty's insistence of talking at odd moments teases the reader away from pure action and prepares the way for a silent drama of truth.

The interchanges between Natty and Ellen intentionally confuse three principal terms – friend, father, and enemy – and thus introduce the romance's central anxiety about the true nature of paternal-filial bonds. Throughout the night, the terms sound their permutations on the open prairie, where it is both imperative and difficult to distinguish friend from foe. Ellen Wade tries to shield her surprise at finding Natty in place of her lover:

> "Oh! I knew you to be a man, and I thought I knew the whine of the hound, too," she answered hastily, as if willing to explain she knew not what and then checking herself, as though fearful of having, already, said too much.
>
> "I saw no dogs, among the teams of your father," the trapper dryly remarked.
>
> "Father!" exclaimed the girl, feelingly, "I have no father! I had nearly said no friend." The old man turned towards her, with a look of kindness and interest, that was even more conciliating than the ordinary, upright, and benevolent expression of his weather-beaten countenance.
>
> "Why then do you venture in a place where none but the strong should come?" he demanded. "Did you not know that, when you crossed the big river, you left a friend behind you that is always bound to look to the young and feeble, like yourself."
>
> "Of whom do you speak?"

"The law – 'tis bad to have it, but, I sometimes think, it is worse, where it is never to be found. Yes – yes, the law is needed, when such as have not the gifts of strength and wisdom are to be taken care of." (36–37)

Having seen Ellen in Ishmael's camp, Natty assumes that the frontiersman is her father and, more fundamentally, that fathers serve as protectors of their children. Ellen's correction and swift interjection ("I had nearly said no friend") immediately challenges those assumptions. In a later segment of the conversation, she furthers the confusion of terms when she responds to Ishmael's approach through the darkness: " 'The family is stirring;' cried Ellen with a tremor in her voice that announced nearly as much terror at the approach of her friends, as she had before manifested at the presence of her enemies" (79).

That the hero of the Leatherstocking tales – the man "driven . . . to seek a final refuge against society in the broad tenantless plains of the west" – should go back on the principles of his life and advocate the protection of the law provides a measure of the danger Cooper feared if paternal affection were not what it appeared. Even Natty seems embarrassed by his step out of character. Ellen's ambiguous position forces him, for all his avoidance of the "law," to recognize his assumptions about the natural laws governing parents and children. In fact, when Ellen starts in fear of Ishmael a second time, Natty's suspicions turn first to Ellen and Paul rather than to Ishmael. Against his evident affection for the young couple, he feels the presumptions of tradition: "I know not what need ye may have, children, to fear those you should both love and honor" (81). The rhetorical allusion to the Fifth Commandment shows that even Natty's individualism depends on basic social assumptions about responsibilities and obligations within the family. The freedom and nobility Natty claims through his alliance with the wilderness are habitually celebrated by his apostrophes to the idealized filial-paternal bond of Chingachgook and Uncas, and, in *The Prairie* specifically, by Hard-Heart's adoption of Natty as his father.

Even more important to the romance as a whole, Natty recognizes that any breakdown in a bond so basic is potentially fatal. In the first scene he immediately extends his own paternal benevolence to Ellen; in the second he warns the couple that "something must be done to save your lives" (81). In the middle of Natty's effort to pin down Ellen's relationship to the patriarch, he hears the click of cocking rifles and pulls the pair to the ground barely in time to avoid "the ragged lead" sent "buzzing within a dangerous proximity of their heads" by Ishmael and his sons (80).

The significance of this paternal volley depends on its double repetition, when actions in the main plot converge on the questions raised in the seemingly digressive discussions between Natty and Ellen Wade. On "a single naked and ragged rock" high over the monotonous prairie, Ishmael's citadel rises in token of his isolation and aggressively asserted domination (116). There, in a quick succession of scenes, the action exposes violence as the ultimate sanction of patriarchal authority. Ishmael's deliberate firing at Ellen Wade, the exposure of Ishmael's and Abiram's kidnapping, and the rebellion of son against father each comment on the other and together precipitate the murder of the patriarch's eldest son.

The uncertainty Ellen Wade feels about her ties to Ishmael stems partly from the blurring of affection and violence in Ishmael's paternal manner. When he first catches sight of Ellen at the summit of the citadel raptly gazing over the prairie, he speaks of her kindly as the "child" and cajoles her with a kind of gruff tenderness that passes for a display of affection within the tribe: "What is it, Nell? . . . Why, Nell, girl, ar' ye deaf? Nell, I say" (120). Yet the moment he suspects that she has played the "prank" on him, he explodes with anger, sparked by the slightest trace of filial disobedience:

> Ishmael struck the breech of his rifle violently on the earth, and shouted in a voice that might easily have been heard by Ellen, had not her attention still continued rapt on the object which so unaccountably attracted her eyes in the distance.
>
> "Nell!" continued the squatter; "away with you, fool! will you bring down punishment on your own head. Why Nell! – she has forgotten her native speech; let us see if she can understand another language."
>
> Ishmael threw his rifle to his shoulder, and at the next moment it was pointed upward at the summit of the rock. Before

time was given for a word of remonstrance, it had sent forth
its contents, in its usual streak of bright flame. Ellen started
like the frightened chamois, and uttering a piercing scream,
she darted into the tent, with a swiftness that left it uncertain
whether terror or actual injury had been the penalty of her
slight offence. (122)

As the rifle shot implies, fatherly affection offers no protection
from the threat of his power nor from the quick fluctuations of
an inherently unstable psyche that Cooper attributed not only
to Ishmael but to the "human volcano" in general (389).

The rifle shot leads directly to the confrontation between Ishmael and his sons by unlocking the "deep impulse and dark
desire" underlying the social bond (Wasserstrom 426). By dis-
playing the actual underpinnings of his authority, Ishmael liberates his sons from their anonymity; for the first time, they
appear as individuals capable of action independent of their father. Ishmael answers their restlessness by explicitly threatening
to enforce filial compliance with deadly force. The exchange is
pivotal to the unarticulated action before and after – to the rifle
shot sent toward one young woman and the unexpected rev-
elation of a second:

> The action of the squatter was too sudden and unexpected to
> admit of prevention, but the instant it was done, his sons
> manifested, in an unequivocal manner, the temper with which
> they witnessed the desperate measure. Angry and fierce glances
> were interchanged, and a murmur of disapprobation was ut-
> tered by the whole in common.
>
> "What has Ellen done, father," said Asa, with a degree of
> spirit, which was the more striking from being unusual, "that
> she should be shot at . . .!"
>
> "Mischief;" deliberately returned the squatter, but with a
> cool expression of defiance in his eye that showed how little
> he was moved by the ill-concealed humour of his children.
> "Mischief, boy; mischief! take you care that the disorder don't
> spread."
>
> "It would need a different treatment in a man, than in yon
> screaming girl!"
>
> "Asa, you ar' a man, as you have often boasted; but re-
> member I am your father, and your better."

"I know it well; and what sort of a father!"

"Harkee, boy . . . Be modest in your speech, my watchful son. . . ."

"I'll stay no longer to be hectored like a child in petticoats. You talk of law, as if you knew of none, and yet you keep me down, as though I had not life and wants of my own to provide for. I'll stay no longer to be treated like one of your meanest cattle." (122–23)

Both Ishmael and his son understand the dispute over Ellen as an impulse toward rebellion. To this point in the narrative, Ishmael's sons have acted as inarticulate extensions of their father's will: the family consists of "Ishmael Bush and his seven sledge-hammer sons" (56). In the opening scene, one of Cooper's most powerful and controlled, the sons appear behind their father, looking like him and like each other, with no distinguishing characteristics. They move only at their father's command and act so instinctively to fulfill his will that they level their patch of cottonwood trees with no more specific orders than a peremptory "be stirring" (25). In such recurring references to the sons as "the tribe of wandering Ishmael," Cooper's Biblical rhetoric steadily refers their lack of individual identity to Ishmael's patriarchal stature.

In their confrontation, Asa takes on individual character by articulating his brothers' dissatisfaction over their subordination. By their anger, they show that the apparent merger with their father's identity has been compelled. They have appeared bovine in their voiceless conformity because Ishmael has treated them as his "meanest cattle." Asa attributes the brothers' subservience to his father's break from society. Although the patriarch has moved to the frontier to escape limitations on his authority and to claim unbridled freedom, he purchases his larger sense of self from his sons. The father's repudiation of "law" yokes the sons to a tyrannous rule (McWilliams 265). For all his boasts of providing the unlimited prairie as a legacy for his sons, he undercuts their accession to manhood. The traditional sanctions of patriarchal authority called up by Ishmael – "I am your father and your better" – keep the younger generation from advancing to manhood. Asa feels he has been kept "like a child in petticoats."

Instead of engendering a multiplying third generation, the sons support their father in the phallic pinnacle of his prairie fortress.

If the rifle shot against Ellen Wade raises the tension between father and son to the surface, the drama's next movement drives to its deepest sources. Interrupting the contention between father and son "which threatened to become still more violent," alarmed cries from the brothers stir Ishmael to "Look!" toward the towering rock where Ellen Wade had stood when he fired (123). But instead of leading Ishmael away from the conflict with Asa, as the younger and more fearful brothers had hoped, the cries swing the patriarch's gaze from his eldest son to the symbolic source of their conflict:

> The squatter turned slowly from his offending son, and cast an eye upward that still lowered with deep resentment. . . .
>
> A female stood on the spot, from which Ellen had been so fearfully expelled. Her person was the smallest size that is believed to comport with beauty, and which poets and artists have chosen as the beau idéal of feminine loveliness. Her dress was of a dark and glossy silk, and fluttered like gossamer around her form. Long, flowing, and curling tresses of hair, still blacker and more shining than her robe, fell at times about her shoulders, completely enveloping the whole of her delicate bust in their ringlets; or at others streaming long and waving in the wind. . . . One small and exquisitely moulded hand was pressed on her heart, while with the other she made an impressive gesture, which seemed to invite Ishmael, if any further violence was meditated, to direct it against her bosom. (123–24)

Cooper's underscoring of Inez's sexuality points to the nature of the competition between Ishmael and Asa – a competition of relative masculine prowess implicit in the son's earlier insistence that he is "a man" and in his father's concurrence that the degree of manhood should determine authority (Wasserstrom 428–29; Porte 47–48). Joel Porte notes Cooper's strategy of moving Inez away from the oedipal taboo by exploiting her youthful and "passionate pubescence" and thus anticipating an American obsession with "nymphet sexuality in our literature from Poe to Nabokov" (48). Yet aspects of the scene carried over from *The Pioneers* – the hasty rifle shot, the anger between competing generations of men, the dark ringlets of their prize, the gesture toward the breast heightened by silence – serve less to dismiss the idea of oedipal conflict than to emphasize once again that in Cooper's work the most basic competition between father and son leaves the issue of the mother deeply buried and plays itself out in boldly sexual terms. Instead of turning on Hamlet's competition with Claudius over a tabooed mother, Cooper's young men contest their manhood over a woman of the son's generation tabooed, though not always as strongly, to the father.

Cooper's mother barely appears in his surviving correspondence, and although we know that he took his young children to visit her at the Mansion House, the most suggestive information we have about their relationship derives from her wish to leave him her family property, his attempt to change his name to Fenimore, and our knowledge that after her death he seemed for a time to feel less closely bound to Cooperstown. These elements of their relationship suggest their importance to each other, but they keep the precise psychological charge in their relationship veiled. On the other hand, we know that Cooper's adult masculine identity was very much tied up in competition with his father-in-law over Susan De Lancey, that he was deeply engaged with his father's memory as he struggled to establish his fitness as a husband, and that these competitions were closely tied up with his writing. To Cooper, tensions between fathers and sons, between generations of men competing for authority, presented themselves as competitions over the son's mate, rather than over the mother, or, at least, these were the conflicts more readily available to Cooper's art.

The sudden appearance of Inez offers further insight into the confrontation between father and son in less psychological, but equally interesting, terms – terms more in keeping with Cooper's particular symbolic method in *The Prairie* of using parallel elements to comment on each other. Appearing in exactly the same spot, Inez and Ellen bracket the confrontation – the "disorder," Ishmael calls it – between the patriarch and his eldest son. Inez's sudden appearance in Ellen's place, presented almost as a sleight of hand, signals an essential parallel between her captivity and the filial condition of Ellen and Ishmael's offspring. Though adopted niece, sons, and captive should fall into different categories, the scene conflates the divisions and links the main action of Ishmael's westward migration with the more melodramatic kidnapping subplot. By this parallel, Cooper connects the undifferentiated bestiality of Ishmael's sons with Inez's enclosed cage, which they are forced to haul across the prairie. In the benighted ignorance forced on them by their father's escape from "human institutions," their filial status has become a captivity (15). Like Inez, they move in darkness under the power of the isolato – the self-exiled Ishmael, "his hand against every man and every man's hand against him," dwelling "over and against all his kinsmen" (Gen. 16: 11–12).[4]

The violence threatened by Ishmael breaks out between Asa and his uncle Abiram, Ishmael's partner in the captivity of Inez and, by extension, in the excessive domination of his sons. Within moments of Inez's appearance, Asa strikes the elder man; within hours Abiram murders Asa in retribution. Indicating where he assigns responsibility, Cooper transfers the name of Abiram, challenger of Moses's motives for leading the Israelites into the wilderness, from the archetypal Biblical rebel to the punishing elder; he gives to the rebellious son the name of King Asa, who "did that which was right in the eyes of the Lord" (Num. 16: 1–12; Deut. 11: 6; 1 Kings 15: 11).

Although Ishmael does not himself pull the trigger, Cooper establishes Abiram as the agent of the patriarch's injunction "that the disorder" among his sons "don't spread" (123; Wassserstrom 430). To voice his brothers' anger, Asa turns to Abiram "instead of braving the resentment of his father, of whose fierce nature, when aroused, he had had too frequent evidence to excite it wantonly" (125). Abiram is clearly a surrogate; though carried out against the uncle, Asa's rebellion weakens "the frail web of authority with which Ishmael had been able to envelop his restless children" (127). Throughout the narrative, Ishmael would like to slough off his responsibility for the kidnapping and all "things done by [Abiram's] advice," but until Ishmael executes his brother-in-law, Abiram hovers near him as a shadow of Ishmael's darker self. For his part, Abiram cowers under the protection of Ishmael's authority and gigantic strength much as the competitiveness between father and son may hide itself under the sanctioned mantle of a father's authority.

From Asa's first challenge of Ishmael's violence against Ellen to the discovery of his corpse, Cooper keeps before us the idea that Asa's violation was less the insult to his uncle than the rebellion against authority. During this section of the narrative, Ishmael is unusually insecure about his command; around "the circle of his silent sons," he looks for signs of support for "their rebellious brother" (165). As the young men brood "over the absence of their elder brother," Ishmael "cast his scowling eyes from one to the other, like a man who was preparing to meet and to repel an expected assault on his authority" (174). At the time Asa strikes Abiram, Ishmael prefers to restore his authority by adopting "that dignity with which the hand of Nature seems to have invested the parental character" (126). Asserting that where "the law of the land is weak, it is right the law of nature should be strong," he assures Abiram that justice will be done (126). But the tale tells us that it is not civilized respect for his authority but the threat of power beneath it that actually ends the rebellion. The sacrifice of Asa functions to preserve Ishmael's control over the family:

> United to their parents by ties no stronger than those which use had created, there had been great danger, as Ishmael had foreseen, that the overloaded hive would quickly swarm, and leave him saddled with the difficulties of a young and helpless brood, unsupported by the exertions of those, whom he had already brought to a state of maturity. The spirit of insubordination, which emanated from the unfortunate Asa, had spread among his juniors, and the squatter had been made painfully to remember the time when, in the wantonness of his youth and vigour, he had, reversing the order of the brutes, cast off his own aged and failing parents, to enter into the world unshackled and free. But the danger had now abated, for a time at least; and if his authority was not restored with all its former influence, it was visibly admitted to exist, and to maintain its ascendancy a little longer. (195–96)

The trick of Ishmael's memory, returning him to his own rebellion against his father, makes the stakes clear. Without the deadly assertion of his authority, perpetrated under the cover of Abiram's crime, the rebellion among his sons would have spread (Grossman 58). Within society, the web of patriarchal authority would have been less "frail," supported by the stronger cables of multiplying interconnections between families. While the overall authority controlling each individual might be greater, it would not be centered at one point and, consequently, its sanction would depend on the more general and regulated power of society rather than on individual power. But because Ishmael broke from his own father and moved westward, he extracted his own authority outside the modifying controls of society and exposed its true nature. Though curbed within society into "the law of the land," the true "law of nature" behind patriarchal authority is the law of competition and power between father and son.

Through Ishmael's relationship to Abiram, Cooper arrives at the seeming contradiction between the threat of patriarchal power and the necessity of creating sufficient authority within society to restrain the competitiveness and violence that isolated men will exercise to expand their sense of self against the anxiety of insignificance – against Thomas Sutpen's boyhood discovery that he and his father counted for nothing (*Absalom* 234–35). The tension between those two aspects of patriarchal authority was to become the focus of Cooper's next book, *The Wept of Wish-Ton-Wish*. In describing how the news of Asa's death ends the rebellion, Cooper discovers the paradigmatic value of Abraham's story that would structure *The Wept*. In the last moment before the brothers once more subordinate their identities to their father's will, they suspect the pioneer patriarch of murdering his first-born:

> His slow-minded sons, even while they submitted to the impressions of the recent event, had glimmerings of terrible distrusts, as to the manner in which their elder brother had met with his death. There were faint and indistinct images in the minds of two or three of the oldest, which portrayed the father himself, as ready to imitate the example of Abraham, without the justification of the sacred authority which commanded the holy man to attempt the revolting office. But then, these images were so transient and so much obscured in the intellectual mists, as to leave no very strong impressions,

> and the tendency of the whole transaction, as we have already
> said, was rather to strengthen than to weaken the authority
> of Ishmael. (196)

Cast from the perspective of the threatened, this may be
Cooper's least qualified indictment of patriarchal authority.
Whether sanctified or not, the threatened enforcement underlying the father's natural command is, at root, a "revolting office." Given the accusing looks of Ishmael's sons, it is difficult
to overlook the pun. The power of the father is "revolting"
both in the sense that it is *abhorrent* to our sense of progression
from one generation to the next, and in the sense that the use
of the father's power to compel obedience *engenders rebellious
thoughts* and the fragmentation Ishmael himself exemplified when
he deserted his mother and father.

In the magnificent trial closing the tale, Ishmael's repudiation
of Abiram enacts, as Wasserstrom noted, the repression of paternal violence Freud described in accounting for the origin of
society. By setting the renunciation on the empty stage of *The
Prairie,* Cooper asserts as strongly as possible that the New
World has no special dispensation from history. To the extent
that a social and political *tabula rasa* can exist, it must always be
scored by the lines of power within the family. Though Ishmael
adopts the forms of bestowing justice on his followers and cap-
tives, his final judgments more crucially redefine his role as patriarch.

For both readers and participants, Ishmael's last demonstration
of his "species of patriarchal power" excites a "degree of awe"
(468–69); Cooper's official explanation – that "the possession
of authority, however it may be abused," is "elevating" – glosses
over the more important origin of that feeling (468). In his capacity as judge, Ishmael brings the latent threat of his power to
the surface. The "self-constituted tribunal" of Ishmael or any
outlaw – the pseudo-trial became a staple of Westerns and
gangster movies – causes terror by evoking those rituals meant
to sanctify the use of force within society and perverting them
to lend authority to individual will. In turn, the bogus trial casts
doubt on institutionalized justice by its power to suggest that
deliberation is but the hesitation of a cat about to pounce. The

unauthorized trial is yet another distorted version of Abraham's sacrifice of Isaac.

As the trial progresses, however, fear gives way to less threatening contemplation, for Ishmael's series of judgments on others enacts his own surrender of uncontrolled power. In his pronouncements, he moves from the kidnapping – the most public display of his power and the most artificial level of Cooper's plot – to the murder of his first-born – the most private and realistically convincing level of the narrative. But Cooper's structure and language continue to connect the two events. Immediately after releasing Inez, Ishmael lashes out against Abiram, planner of the kidnapping and the yet undetected murderer of his son; speaking of Inez, he concedes that "it was a mistake to take a child from its parent" (470). Evidently, he has come to understand the kidnapping by meditating on his own loss.

By allowing Ellen Wade to choose whether to go with Paul Hover or remain under his care, Ishmael limits his authority to the familial sphere. Though he has tried to command her sexuality – he "had calculated to make [her] one day a daughter of [his] own" – he sets aside his authority as "a ruler of inclinations" (475, 477). In keeping with Cooper's sense that less oppressive command creates a stronger bond, Ellen initially feels more tightly bound to Ishmael by his decision to release her. For the first time, she fully expresses her obligation to him: "You took me a fatherless, impoverished and friendless orphan, . . . may Heaven in its goodness bless you for it" (478). Only when the patriarch surrenders the arbitrary use of his superior power can the bonds of reciprocal duty and obligation become the basis of familial and social cohesion: in the terms set by *The Prairie,* the Fifth Commandment's call to filial duty can only function when supported by the injunction of the Sixth Commandment against murder.

At the opening of the trial, Ishmael speaks to Abiram as if to disassociate himself from the promptings of his own psyche: "Peace! . . . Your voice is like a raven's in my ears. If *you* had never spoken I should have been spared this shame" (470). Though he cannot acknowledge his own guilt in his son's murder, as he did in the case of the kidnapping, Ishmael expresses no surprise when Natty Bumppo reveals Abiram as the killer.

At an unacknowledged level, his automatic acceptance signals the link of the kidnapping and murder, and the joint desire of father and surrogate to maintain control over the seven sons.

Ishmael's solitary deliberations over Abiram's fate enact his repudiation of that side of his nature manifest in Abiram's surrogate filicide. To cast out Abiram, Ishmael distances himself by again taking on the rhetoric of Biblical judgment. But despite his exterior aloofness, Ishmael cannot entirely repress the internal kinship between them. Looking back for the last time toward the narrow ledge of rock where Ishmael has left Abiram to be his "own executioner," he saw the blasted willow and "even traced the still upright form of the being he had left to his misery": "Turning the roll of the swell he proceeded with the feelings of one, who had been suddenly and violently separated from a recent confederate, forever" (494–95).

With remarkable control, Cooper moves from the visible symbol of Ishmael's repudiation to the inner wrenching Ishmael feels at the loss, and finally to his changed perception of the prairie itself. Repudiating, through Abiram, the unchecked power of his will, he feels his sudden vulnerability:

> For the first time, in a life of so much wild adventure, Ishmael felt a keen sense of solitude. The naked prairies began to assume the forms of illimitable and dreary wastes, and the rushing of the wind sounded like the whisperings of the dead. It was not long before he thought a shriek was borne past him on a blast. . . . The teeth of the squatter were compressed, and his huge hand grasped the rifle, as though it would crush the metal like paper. Then came a lull, a fresher blast, and a cry of horror that seemed to have been uttered at the very portals of his ears. A sort of echo burst involuntarily from his own lips, as men will often shout under unnatural excitement, and throwing his rifle across his shoulder, he proceeded towards the rock with the strides of a giant. (496)

Though he struggles to deny his identification with Abiram's crime – an identification registered by the compulsive grasping of his rifle – the involuntary groan betrays him. With the death of his brother-in-law, a part of his nature escapes as if he had been delivered of a possessing demon. But even more prominent is Ishmael's new sense of solitude. Though Cooper has repeatedly directed his readers to the dreariness of the plains, Ishmael first feels "the frailty of existence and the fulfillment of time," etched by the silhouette of the gallows tree, only when he surrenders the ruthless control Abiram represented (486–87). Solitude descends on him when he can no longer feel a society unto himself. Cooper exposes the patriarch's domination of his tribe as a strategy for shielding himself from the essential limitations of his condition. By controlling his sons and their futures, he felt immune to death and age and empowered over nature; in the opening scene his sons sunk their axes into the cottonwood trees, seeming to make nature their victim. Until the loss of Abiram, he had read the stage of Cooper's tale as a vast reflector of his own will. Now he faces nature's enduring indifference – he sees, in its "empty wastes" and "masses of rock," "an ancient country, incomprehensibly stripped of its people" (486).

By reversing the order of Ishmael's march and sending him eastward at the moment Abiram's crime is apprehended and judged, Cooper equates the entire westward journey with Abiram's influence and Ishmael's patriarchal power. The circumscription of the filicidal threat, signaled by Abiram's death, essentially ends Ishmael's identity as the frontier patriarch: for that reason, he alone of the principal characters is "never heard of more" (498). He returns eastward, where his patriarchal herds are "blended among a thousand others" (498). Read in an optimistic light, his disappearance shows how society functions to curb the unchecked sway of patriarchal authority; but read in the darker spirit of his last nocturnal vigil, Ishmael's disappearance is less an unqualified defeat of the father's power than a charting of its course underground.

Satanstoe: The Paradigm of Change and Continuity

On his return from Europe in 1833 after an absence of seven years, Cooper endured a profound shock to his identity as a national writer. The outward symptoms were obvious: – a severe decline in sales, a decision – later revoked – to give up writing fiction, an inability to settle comfortably in New York, renewed financial difficulties, and finally the remove to Cooperstown in 1836. To his American contemporaries, Cooper may have seemed simply a novelist returning after too long an absence abroad, but in Cooper's mind he returned a more seasoned father, ready to receive filial respect. The full sting of Cooper's alienation originated in his disappointed expectations.

Cooper had left America with the accolades of his contemporaries, and in general his seven years in Europe supported his confidence as a father and writer. In Europe, his wife and five children had been dependent solely on him, and he had evidently taken satisfaction in arranging schools and personally guiding their peripatetic introduction to European life and arts. Among Europeans he had made friends with people of high standing whose interest confirmed his coveted role as an American spokesman. Among Americans abroad, he had cultivated both the artists and the first prosperous pioneers of the reverse migration studied by Henry James. The young sculptor Horatio Greenough had become a particularly close friend, and their frank letters suggest that Cooper had found in Europe support analogous to that he had found among his friends in the Bread and Cheese: a combination of friendship and barely stated deference to his seniority and established success. After dedicating himself to the intense study of European society and government in three novels, *The Bravo* (1831), *The Heidenmauer* (1832), and *The Headsman* (1833), and many volumes of travel journals, Cooper had expected Americans to greet him as a wiser father – a more commanding authority. He had, after all, fulfilled his paternal duty – *Notions of the Americans* (1828) was a vigilant defense of his young country against European cynicism and condescension. Now it was up to America to reciprocate and accord him filial respect.

Yet even before his return, the signs of trouble were clear. Taking its lead from the very English critics Cooper had attacked for their excessive influence on American intellectual life, the New York press had been scornful of *Notions,* and they had not read his European novels (*Letters* 1: xxiii–xxiv; Dekker 134). He had been deeply wounded by the U.S. government's seemingly perverse promotion of a diplomat who had defended France against Cooper's criticism of French mistreatment of America during the Finance Controversy. Even before he left Paris, he felt himself the "object of constant attacks in the American papers" (Dekker 140; *Letters* 2: 383).

Frustrated as Cooper often was during the years following his return, perhaps no American writer of his time was better constituted to survive virulent opposition. Cooper knew how to fight for his identity. If readers would not accept his paternal authority as a novelist, he would adapt and force it on them as a political columnist in the angry tones of a chiding father. For five years he wrote no romances. In *A Letter to His Countrymen* (1834), he lashed out at the power of the Whig press, the general disregard for the Constitution, and the country's cultural insensitivity, particularly to art and literature produced by Americans. He satirized New York society and its "greedy rapacity for money" in *The Monikins* (1835) (*Letters* 3: 233); from 1834 to 1836, he wrote an anonymous political column in the Democratic *Evening Post* edited by William Cullen Bryant; and in 1838 he published *The American Democrat,* which he hoped would be adopted by New York public schools as a text. In these years a reviewer's snide comment – "This last work of Mr. Cooper [*A Letter to His Countrymen*] treats of himself and the Constitution of the United States" – became unintentionally apt (*Letters* 3: 7). His defense of American principles carries the emotional force of a man defending his identity as a founder.

Born in the year of the Constitution's ratification, Cooper preserved an immediate sense of the experimental nature of his country. In 1830 he had witnessed the unsuccessful attempts of his friend Lafayette and other European liberals to institute republican governments; he saw no guarantee of America's survival. Even after the country seemed secure from foreign attack, the question of internal stability remained. In his letters, Cooper comments as early as the 1820s on the possibility of a violent confrontation between North and South over nullification. Living abroad, he realized sooner than his countrymen that England and other European countries would not be disappointed if the rising power of the new nation were broken by civil war. When he returned to the United States and saw the party of "brokers and bankers" discounting the importance of constitutional principles, he felt bound to warn the nation (*Letters* 4: 489).

When Cooper's political writing brought additional attacks and failed to provide enough money to bring up five children, Cooper felt the full blow of his altered status. To recoup his emotional forces and secure a more stable financial position, he retreated to Cooperstown and rebuilt his father's house. The famous battle with his neighbors over picnicking rights at Three-Mile Point was less an exercise in filial duty than a symptom of his own effort to fall back on the support of his father's authority as a base from which he could resume his career as a novelist.

Under these pressures, control became the major requirement of Cooper's psyche, and his imagination was rich enough to develop several strategies for achieving it. One was to escape with Natty Bumppo to the wilderness – to resist social control by submitting to the stoic self-discipline and necessity of a person in the most unmediated relationship with Providence. Another was to mount an unrelenting rear-guard action: increasingly faced with irreversible changes in American society, Cooper fought back – often on the ludicrously chosen ground of his libel suits – to maintain the illusion of exerting some influence on cultural forces. A third strategy was to imagine a world in which a man like himself might achieve a dominating position. It was a combination of his need to imagine reintegration with his country and his desire to understand how history had transformed America into a place so alien that prompted his return to the frontier scenario in *The Littlepage Manuscripts,* the most ambitious historical work of his later career.

The particular donnée for this four-generation family chronicle was a local controversy over tenants' rights that spread to four New York counties in the upper Hudson Valley in the early 1840s. Dubbed, somewhat hyperbolically, the Anti-Rent Wars, the disorder and violence seemed to Cooper symptomatic of the destructive tendencies in American society as a whole. Though his avowed purpose was to trace the origins of "the Anti-Rent commotion that now exists among us, and which certainly threatens the destruction of our system," the first and finest volume, *Satanstoe,* is more accurately an effort to re-imagine the origins of American history and create a past that spared the nation and its citizens the disruption and alienation Cooper and many of his fellow writers experienced in the 1830s and 1840s (*Letters* 5: 7; Ringe, "Cooper's Littlepage Novels").

As the central coordinates of his plot, Cooper seized on both the political dimension of independence – the separation from England – and the geographic dimension – the extension of the first European settlements from the Atlantic coast into the transforming American wilderness. Quite literally charting the development of his young hero on these coordinates of independence, Cooper proposed a less radical explanation for America's Revolution in the form of an alternative founding legend. His central metaphors for examining the issues of political authority were once again the patterns of authority within a patriarchal family and the settlement of the frontier. But the obvious similarities stopped there. In the Littlepage trilogy, the specific patterns of authority and the process of settlement are entirely different from those he described in earlier accounts of the patriarch. *Satanstoe* focuses on the son rather than the father and on the easy transition of authority from one generation to the next. Cooper's ideal model of American development reconciles the tensions between the negative and positive views of the frontier patriarch: between the costs of patriarchal egotism and the need for patriarchal protection, between distrust of excessive patriarchal control and his admiration for the organic society engendered by the responsible assertion of patriarchal will.

Satanstoe's account of provincial colonial life is frankly nostalgic without being sentimental. By looking away from contemporary society momentarily, Cooper was able to lower his defensive guard and succeeded in transforming his own bitter feelings of rejection into the naïvely startled confusion of his narrator. In his first utterance to the reader, Corny Littlepage posits change as the primary condition of American life: "It is easy to foresee that this country is destined to undergo great and rapid changes" (9). Then, launching into the familial metaphors that structure the entire trilogy, he gives voice to the unsettling implications of finding oneself in such a world:[1]

> . . . should the next twenty years do as much as the last, toward substituting an entirely new race for the descendants of our own immediate fathers, it is scarcely too much to predict that even these traditions [of colonial society] will be lost in the whirl and excitement of a throng of strangers. (9)

According to Corny's central image, the rapidity of change breaks the family line and severs past from future. The disoriented man of the present sees himself replaced by future generations he recognizes only as a "throng of strangers." Cut off from past and present he is left alone, and, unlike Lewis's Adam, he is not "happily bereft of ancestry" (5). Living in America's rapidly changing society confronted individuals with the brevity and insignificance of their own lives.

Cooper thus predicates his narrative on a central problem of republican theory. In *The Rights of Man* (1791), Paine's definition of natural rights extols the freedom of each new generation in precisely the terms Corny finds so unsettling:

> All men are born equal, and with equal and natural rights, and in the same manner as if posterity had been conceived by creation instead of generation . . . and consequently every child being born into it must be considered as deriving its existence from God. The world is as new to him as it was to the first man that existed, and his natural right in it is of the

same kind. Each generation must be as free to act for itself
. . . as the age and generations which preceded it. (40)

Emerson would translate the republican claim in Cooper's
own time, insisting we should "also enjoy an original relation
to the universe" (3). But to Cooper's hero, Emerson's injunction
that "We must go alone" is more bewildering than inspiring
(71). Although Corny's adventures follow his efforts to throw
off the disadvantages of unequal colonial status, the impulse in-
itiating his narrative of gradual liberation wells up from his sense
that the society now granting his freedom has failed to fulfill
an equal, if opposite, need. As Montesquieu asserted, "All history proves man's instinctive reluctance to be alone, his desire
if imprisoned alone in a dungeon to cultivate the friendship of
the spiders" (qtd. in Fliegelman 24). Corny found an American
society that had deepened rather than alleviated the individual's
loneliness.

Corny writes from an imprecisely defined time in the 1760s
or 1770s, but through him Cooper voices the anxieties of his
own America. Corny anticipates Tocqueville's frequent refrain
of loneliness amidst the crowd, which, through the mediation
of Southern apologists like Fitzhugh and Calhoun, provided
many of the materials for Marx's attack on capitalist society and
its treatment of individuals as separate nomads. Like Cooper,
Tocqueville saw the instability of the family as both symptom
and perpetuating cause of the individual's isolation; Corny
Littlepage confronts the anxieties of democracy in Jacksonian
America (Meyers 24–75):

> Among democratic nations new families are constantly
> springing up, others are constantly falling away, and all that
> remain change their condition; the woof of time is every instant
> broken, and the track of generations effaced. Those who went
> before are soon forgotten; of those who will come after no
> one has any idea. (*Democracy* 2: 99)

Cooper's choice of first-person narration perfectly met the
demands of his historical inquiry and of his personal response
to contemporary American society: he took full advantage of
the personal memoir's informing impulse "to discover, defend,
assert and manufacture the self" (Spacks 313). In exploiting the

autobiographical form, Cooper not only describes the American's discovery of an independent self during the closing decades of the colonial period, but also expresses the narrator's need, at the point of retrospection, to defend his self against the atomized society threatening him with insignificance, to assert the community of voices in the crowd, and, at least within his own family, to give substance to that community – to constitute it. Having witnessed by his own process of growing up the decisive turning point in colonial thinking from dependence to independence, Corny writes his autobiographical narrative with both civic and personal motives. As a citizen, he hopes that his family's history will be a modest antidote to the obliterating effects of change. On a more personal and less conscious level, Corny reaches back to a time of more stable relationships between individual and society – before Americans gave up the security of their dependent provincial status as the price of their freedom. By committing the continuation of the family narrative to his son and grandson, he hopes to forge his narrative of the past into a link with the future; by making his retrospective narrative a legacy to his heirs, he hopes to give his own life continuity and meaning.

Concerned with both stability and historical change, Cooper produced the major work of his later career by combining the novel of manners with the historical novel as he had adapted it over the course of his career from Sir Walter Scott (Dekker). Scott's hero typically finds himself poised between a society on the verge of extinction and its more powerful and crass replacement – in Cooper's adaptation of the Waverly formula, Corny perches uncertainly between two views of himself. Although the retrospective opening of *Satanstoe* lets it be known that the cozy society of old New York will give way to progressive history as inevitably as did the clans of Scotland, in the body of the narrative provincial society shines forth in its barely cracked coherence. Skillfully handling the autobiographical form, Cooper claims representative status for Corny as he wavers between his original Loyalist habits of thought and his discomforting, and at first barely conscious sense, that his allegiances are shifting from England to his native ground.

In an America of rapid and continual change, the narrator of

Satanstoe cannot assume a shared understanding of manners with his audience. In fact, unless he commits his history to paper, he assumes that nothing of the thoughts and usages of his own world will be passed down. Therefore, *Satanstoe* focuses less on the tension between individual will and social manners, as a Jane Austen novel might, than on re-creating a society in which principles are passed on through the nurturing medium of shared customs. In *Satanstoe,* Cooper escapes the doctrinaire and abrasive polemic that cut such a large swath through many of his late novels by finding a form in which even the most relaxed recollection of drinking punch at the fireside carries forward his political purpose: to persuade people emotionally of the value of social cohesion and continuity. If American literature of the Adamic tradition evokes a world of individuals bound only by voluntary covenants, *Satanstoe* celebrates an organic society of families in which social obligations are assumed as a matter of custom.

In an odd way, Cooper's family chronicle, for all its eighteenth-century habits of style, gives voice to a more persistent American problem than the more dominant strain of family novels like *The House of the Seven Gables, Absalom, Absalom!,* or *Go Down, Moses.* To simplify greatly, the young heroes of these later novels, while fascinated by the past, at least believe they are trying to escape it. Although *Satanstoe* follows the young hero's quest for independence, it is motivated by his concern as an adult that Americans have no connection with the past to escape. And that concern leads to an attempt to forge a link between past and present. Whereas Ike McCaslin cannot free his mind from the ledgers of his grandfather, the later heroes of the Littlepage trilogy seem barely to have skimmed Corny Littlepage's bequeathed manuscript and have only the vaguest notion of how their fathers lived.

The crowning flourish of Cooper's literary strategy is his chatty and uncharacteristically relaxed tone. Only in the wickedly gossipy letters to his wife does Cooper so fully reveal his good spirits. Nothing could bring out more effectively the feeling of social cohesion Cooper intended than Corny Littlepage's easy confidence that we'll share his provincial assumptions. We smile at his naïveté, yet our very superiority acknowledges our loss of shared values so confidently held. The pleasure Corny takes in narrating his adventures and documenting the milieu of his early years entirely lacks the self-pity that spoils the last volume of the Littlepage Manuscripts and crops up in later nostalgic narrators like Cather's Jim Burden. Corny's fondness for the past comes from no sense of having failed in the present. The feelings of isolation and loneliness haven't yet dragged him down into cynicism or even sadness. They spring from the very first instant of crisis before even the strongest person has time to respond with heroism or bitterness and feels only vulnerable confusion: What's going wrong? So Cooper must have felt when he first sensed he could no longer count on his American audience.

In his understanding of the responsibilities of the novelist, Cooper generally followed a sensational model (Fliegelman 9–35). In *Satanstoe,* Cooper recaptures his confidence in the power of descriptive prose to persuade politically as well as aesthetically. Like Rousseau's father, Cooper would lead his readers through a world where their experience would be manipulated programmatically by the invisible hand of the paternal artist until the reader's natural impulses and gradually schooled reason would evolve and comprehend the principles holding society together. Given the Lockean primacy of sensation, artists in control of their readers' sensations would also control the formation of their readers' selves. Evocative description of a coherent society would create citizens capable of creating that society.

In *Satanstoe,* the education of Corny Littlepage and his emergence as both a fit successor to his father and a future developer of the frontier becomes the governing metaphor for Cooper's imagined ideal of national development. In the late eighteenth century of Cooper's childhood, Americans formulated their social interdependence by imagining each individual at the center of a series of snug concentric spheres. Surrounded first by family, then by town or village, then by country, the individual felt securely related to his world and his God. It was almost as if the Ptolemaic universe had been called back to mediate the stresses and isolation in a social world ruled by the forces of

Newtonian physics. In a 1780 letter, Abigail Adams reminded her son John Quincy of his true place in the world:

> . . . every new mercy you receive is a new debt upon you, a new obligation to a diligent discharge of the various relations in which you stand connected; in the first place, to your great Preserver; in the next, to society in general; in particular, to your country, to your parents, and to yourself. (1: 147)

The letter emphasizes expanding duties to society, but through the mother's strict demands emerge the psychic benefits of such bold confidence in the individual's significance. Humble as she petitions her son to be, he is an essential cog in his universe at all levels. An individual could travel to the farthest limits of such a world without ever extending beyond his connections – without ever being alone.[2]

Cooper plays out the relationship of father and son, his central historical metaphor, by organizing his narrative around the young hero's gradually widening cyclical journeys out from the family into the enveloping circles of society. On these journeys, Corny Littlepage grows into an independent American. In the tradition of the epic of the son, popularized in the eighteenth century by Fénelon's *Telemachus* (1699), Cooper charts Corny's increasing independence from his father. As Sterne wrote in defending the educational value of the grand tour, traveling brought to culmination the creation of an independent self. Experience of the world and the variety of humors makes us "look into ourselves and form our own" (Sterne 4: 242; Fliegelman 61). Cooper set Corny's education at the deciding historical moment of England's unsuccessful campaign against the French at Ticonderoga in 1757, and in his travels Corny learns crucial lessons about his society that make him take note of his assumptions and so become aware of his uniquely American self.

At the opening of *Satanstoe,* Cooper outlines Corny's relationship with his father. The outward signs of paternal authority, repeatedly emphasized in *The Wept,* are almost totally absent. The change reflects the shift in the meaning of *govern* from a "synonym for rule" toward "its root sense: 'to steer,' 'guide,' 'direct,' and 'regulate' " (Fliegelman 13). Heathcote governed his family by precept and by placing his community in awe of his authority; the senior Littlepage adopts the indirect methods of the Lockean father, manipulating his son's experience to expose him to profitable examples at suitable stages of his development.

Cooper's early scenes establish the mutual affections of father and son; according to Locke and his instructional followers, Chesterfield and Gregory, paternal authority rested not on unquestioned power but on esteem; it was proved less by awe than by affection. By the time we meet young Corny, he has grown beyond the child's need for strict and unexplained discipline. The strength of his father's authority is measured not by the respectful distance between father and son but by their warm friendship. Within this affectional model, the greatest potential difficulty was, as Fliegelman points out, in allowing "children, at an appropriate moment, to leave the parental roof [so that the] new and greater family [might] be made possible" (83). Satanstoe opens with a family debate over whether the time has come for Corny Littlepage to leave home and begin his independent education.

In Satanstoe, leaving the paternal roof does not imply a betrayal of the hero's forefathers, nor is moving to the frontier associated with rebellion. If The Wept, like Hawthorne's "Endicott and the Red Cross," proposed that "the American character was established on narrow lines – through an act of exclusion rather than through absorption," then Satanstoe offers an alternative ideal where national character evolves less by exclusion than by a process of regulated cultural absorption (Bell 58). Cooper allows Corny and his friend Dirck Van Valkenburgh to depart "from beneath the paternal roof" in "high good-humor" because in Satanstoe the role of the father is dispersed throughout society (55). Through the stages of his journey to manhood, Corny travels with a series of men acting as surrogate fathers. Even as he separates from his own father, their presence allows Corny continued access to the values of the older generation and so guarantees continuity from one generation to the next. Corny's parents permit him to enter the world early and often, which in Locke's view was the only satisfactory way to make individuals strong enough to preserve worthy values against temptation: "The only Fence against the World, is a thorough Knowledge of it; into which a young Gentleman should be enter'd by degrees, as he can bear it; and the earlier the better, so he be in safe and skillful Hands to guide him" (73). Corny's surrogate fathers provide the exposure, if not always the safety and skill.

The dispersal of authority among many surrogates frees Corny, as a son, from the exclusive, potentially oppressive authority a father like Heathcote wielded over his community. As Greven observed in assessing the authority of fathers in different family patterns, paternal authority over children is limited in proportion to the children's alternative relationships with other members of their community. If, as Locke advised, the goal of education is defined in part as achieving independence from the exclusive example of one's father or any other single, inevitably flawed, exemplum, the number of Corny's surrogates increases his chances of comparing the merits of different authorities. In the process, Cooper allies American independence, not with filial disrespect and civil war, but with a degree of maturity without which a son's loyalty would be infantile and unworthy of the parent country's respect.

Sustaining the familial metaphor at all levels, Cooper evaluates the various elements of colonial culture and their potential contribution to an independent American identity by assessing the performance of Corny's surrogate fathers. Each of them represents a distinct aspect of old New York. Do they fulfill their paternal responsibilities to Corny, to their own children, to the military or civilian communities they direct? By so consistently using the familial metaphor, Cooper probes the historical shift in consciousness among Americans without breaking the relatively carefree and secure tone of the novel.

Both dominant cultures of colonial New York, the English and the Dutch, are represented at the Littlepage hearthside. Corny's mother is of Dutch descent and his father is inevitably accompanied by a Dutch double, his lifelong friend Colonel Van Valkenburgh. A phlegmatic man, content to sit by the fire with a cup of punch and his pipe, he's the chosen listener to Mr. Littlepage's eleven-minute orations, and his son Dirck is Corny's best childhood friend. Although Colonel Van Valkenburgh is of sterling character and good judgment, Cooper faults him for his lackadaisical ideas about education. On a cultural level, the Colonel's failure to educate his son foreshadows the surprisingly small part Dutch culture would play in post-Revolutionary New York.

The Dutch father sees no need to send his son to college, being "quite content," as Corny notes, "that his son and heir know no more than he knew himself, after making proper allowances for the differences in years and experience" (41). In the last clause, which Corny voices as a reasonable qualification, Cooper ironically comments on Dirck's ignorance; his father complacently hopes that he'll attain, eventually, that remarkable level of articulation expressed through the puffing of his own Dutch pipe. To this failure of education, Cooper humorously attributes the end of the Van Valkenburgh line. Because of his lack of education, Dirck is particularly susceptible to superstition, becomes obsessed by a fortune teller's prediction that he will never marry, and dies a bachelor. By the second half of the novel, Dirck becomes so subdued that he seems invisible. Cooper, like Irving before him, saw in the Dutch admirable generosity, solidity, sensuousness, and harmony with the land that potentially offered a counterforce to the more aggressive Yankee components of American culture. But without education, father and son drop from the same leaden mold; adaptation to social change is impossible. Colonel Van Valkenburgh's paternal failure represents the cultural inflexibility that carried Dutch culture nearly to extinction in Cooper's America.

As Cooper intended to record the change in provincial attitudes toward England, Corny's education focuses primarily on the English elements of his culture. Among his surrogate fathers, Englishmen and Anglophiles predominate. If, in the climate of the late eighteenth and early nineteenth century, Christian examples could be found among the pagan lands of Rasselas's adventures, so Corny Littlepage could learn American truths from Englishmen and Tories. Initially, Corny's insights into the limitations of paternal figures are particularized; he spots the failure of the man without extending the particular exemplum to the entire colonial context. But unconsciously the particular failures prepare for more significant and more conscious shifts in attitude. From early in the narrative, for example, Corny observes the marked contrast between the Anglican divine's arduous attention to the forms and ceremonies of Sunday offices and his weekday pleasure in gamecocks and cards. When the Reverend Mr. Worden (*Word*en, not Worthy) undertakes to keep a "fatherly eye" on Corny and Dirck in Albany, he instead participates in their schemes "with boyish eagerness" (271, 187). His obvious inadequacies teach Corny the wholesome lesson that his elders do not automatically deserve respect; because the man voices Anglophile pieties more often than he does religious ones, Corny unconsciously prepares himself to extend that caution toward the parent state as well.

Corny's association with his future father-in-law, Herman Mordaunt, is far more complex and reflects Cooper's difficulties with Peter De Lancey from the less contentious perspective supplied by the passage of twenty years. Through Corny's admiration for Mordaunt, Cooper captures the strong appeal that the Tory vision of America held out to moderate colonials. Because of his connections to Westchester County, where a closely bound society temporarily split into opposed camps of Loyalists and Rebels, and because of his divided feelings about rebellion, Cooper is unique among major American writers in creating the attractiveness of colonial status to members of the gentry.

Mordaunt is a native-born American, the son of a titled Englishman who recouped his ebbing fortune by an expedient marriage to a New York heiress of Dutch descent. Possessed of sufficient fortune and a large tract of wilderness land, Mordaunt hopes to reverse his own father's strategy by marrying his daughter to the son of an English aristocrat. The American theme did not wait for Henry James. The Mordaunt family history offers a reminder that James tapped the historical as well as the psychological issues of the American romance. In the colony, Herman Mordaunt's unusually wide experience stands out. Where the Littlepages represent the secure but limited provincialism of colonial life, Mordaunt encompasses the full range and contrasts of colonial experience – true of early America as it was later of India or Africa (McClure 1–8). He converses fluently at the elegant table of his Manhattan townhouse; with equal ability, he organizes a wilderness settlement and personally defends it from Indian attack. While Corny's own father is already troubled by gout, his future father-in-law is in full possession of his powers. Even Corny's uncle, a New York lawyer of radical leanings, admits that his political opposite "has talents, a good education, a very handsome estate, and is well-connected in the colony, certainly; some say at home, also" (88). In complimenting him, the lawyer clarifies those financial, social, and familial interests that define the Tory class and its appeal: he is triumphantly "well-connected."

Around the Tory's connectedness, Cooper had to maneuver with some care. Since he wanted to describe the evolution of a cohesive as well as an independent society, his hero had to preempt or refashion, rather than reject, this aspect of Herman Mordaunt's appeal. From their first meeting, Corny recalls, Mordaunt "appeared to be the highest-bred man I had ever seen" (87). He never falters in his admiration for his father-in-law's manners, intelligence, and command – in short, for his patriarchal stature – but his feelings about Mordaunt's political views change considerably when he feels the consequences of living under his particular style of authority.

In an early episode of the book, Corny accepts Herman Mordaunt's opinions about American society without question. To the older man, America is an extension of England: the development of the wilderness is an economic opportunity unavailable "at home." Like his mother's fortune, it will serve to support the Mordaunt line. As a consequence of these interests, he never considers that developing the wilderness might affect the nature of colonial society or necessitate a readjustment of the relationship between England and America. As Mordaunt guides the young Littlepage toward his estate in the countryside of upper Manhattan, they converse about the future of America. Mordaunt speculates in English terms: "I dare say, that in time, both towns and seats will be seen on the banks of the Hudson, and a powerful and numerous nobility to occupy the last" (131). Corny doesn't bat an eye; of course there will be an aristocracy on the Hudson.

Corny's complaisance initially blinds him to the personal disadvantages such an extension of English society would imply. However, when he falls in love with Mordaunt's daughter, Anneké, the father unwittingly educates Corny in the liabilities of colonial status. Without consulting Anneké's opinion, Mordaunt opens negotiations with the father of an English nobleman stationed with a regiment in New York. Even after Corny rescues Anneké from sure death on the disintegrating ice floes of the Hudson, in one of Cooper's most harrowing action sequences, Mordaunt feels only a slight twinge and continues to advance the suit of his titled friend. With wonderfully smug fraternal benevolence toward Corny, his English competitor, Major Bulstrode, accounts for his favored status with the confidence of an older brother blessed by primogeniture. To win the American girl's hand, he counts on breeding, money, and connections: all of which he refers "to the father: and, I can tell you, my fine fellow, that fathers are of some account, in the arrangement of marriages between parties of any standing" (264). He goes on to spell out that Herman Mordaunt "likes my offers of settlement; he likes my family; he likes my rank, civil and military; and I am not altogether without the hope, that he likes *me*" (265).

Faced with these obstacles, Corny begins to understand essential differences between his assumptions and those of Englishman and Tory alike. To win Anneké's hand, Corny can offer only that element of Bulstrode's persuasive catalogue he condescends to place last: "*me*." And in a society that, as he has pointedly learned, recognizes merit reluctantly by restricting its reward according to social position, Corny must, in essence, overturn the decisive power of the father and bring his older brother on an equal footing with himself. In facing these difficulties, he begins to recognize how "American" he is.

Both Corny Littlepage's father and Herman Mordaunt practice benevolent, behind-the-scenes control. To initiate the boys to their adult responsibilities, Mr. Littlepage and Colonel Van Valkenburgh plan their sons' trip to Albany where they are to sell surplus stock from their two farms. It is one of the triumphs of Cooper's lighter touch in *Satanstoe* that Corny Littlepage, as narrator, remains oblivious to the fathers' manipulation. With considerable braggadocio, he and Dirck mishandle the sale. But as the fathers anticipated, market conditions under army occupation are so favorable that even the boys' poor bargain brings

adequate returns. Yet Cooper calls into question Herman Mordaunt's efforts to manipulate his daughter. Although Corny's
criticisms of his future father-in-law must be taken with a grain
of salt, Cooper backs up Corny's concern that Mordaunt has
taken Anneké to the wilderness to allow Major Bulstrode continued opportunities to press his suit during the campaign against
the French. Without doubting the father's benevolence, Cooper
questions the wisdom of leading Anneké into easily avoidable
danger. Mordaunt's aristocratic assumptions place too much
emphasis on marriage to wealth and rank. Operating within a
fixed hierarchical scale opens paternal authority to abuse.

Corny completes his education into the uncertainty of colonial
dependence during the brief but disastrous campaign against
Ticonderoga (Dekker 225–26). Some critics have dismissed
Corny's participation in the English debacle as a boy's lark, and
there is a disconcerting distance between the boy's consciousness
of the event as an occasion for personal courage and the bungling
carnage Cooper simultaneously exposes. Yet the incident is
crucial to the historical novel. In all great historical fiction we
feel a reciprocal relationship between history and the fictional
life of individual characters. Part of the pleasure of reading comes
from our work as detectives trying to follow the novelist as he
works out this reciprocity. The surest sign of bad historical fiction is its absence. Historical events, like the Jacobite Rebellion
or Napoleon's occupation of Moscow, intrude on the lives of
the characters. We see the changes produced by this intrusion
at an intimate level, and, because of the characters' representative
stature, we see how changes in the lives of ordinary people in
turn affect the larger events of history. Corny's meeting with
Lord Howe marks one of those moments when Cooper's "low-
ly" history, made up of "humbler matters" – "the feelings, incidents, and interests of what is purely private life" – brushes
against the great figures of traditional history recorded by "the
Tacituses of former ages" (10).

In Lord Howe, Corny found a man who fulfilled his paternal
responsibilities and thus, as a representative of the king, presented the monarchy in the most favorable light. Gliding by
bateau across Lake George, he invited Corny to join his advance
guard and generously talks to the inexperienced volunteer about

the difficulty of freeing the mind of recollections of home on the eve of battle. His kindness and care extended to all his troops. Looking back on that day, Corny admiringly noted, "My Lord Howe . . . was grave and thoughtful, as became a man who held the lives of others in his keeping, though he was neither depressed nor doubting" – both characteristics of Cooper's failed patriarchs (340). Here was an England that took seriously its responsibilities to the colonies.

Yet, with the brutal arbitrariness Cooper often observed in war, Corny's protector is killed in the first exchange of fire. Without Howe, and Howe's understanding of America, the principal commander fatally blunders – a failure Cooper attributes to his inability to adapt to American conditions. The scene takes only a few pages, but the Americans learn that, despite good men like Howe, they cannot count on the paternal care of England. Dependence leaves too much to chance; one shot leaves them in the hands of a bad servant, victims of a monarch's abrogation of paternal responsibility (Locke 35, 45). Americans would have to give up the security of worthy external authorities like Howe in order to free themselves from the dangers of the incompetent. On the nocturnal retreat across Lake George, a British officer cynically acknowledges the change of attitude toward England after defeat: "On my word, gentlemen, you will have many wonders to relate, when you get back into the family circle" (358). For the first time in *Satanstoe,* the image of an American "family circle" is put in opposition to the English presence in America. England is no longer portrayed as the paternal head of a family extending to the colony. The American family is a separate entity.

At Ticonderoga, Corny witnesses the limit of a British authority, which Cooper places on geographic coordinates. In Manhattan the British are confident of their supremacy, and the people welcome them as the cream of society; in the wilderness, colonials more self-consciously aware of their American status see the British troops as defeated foreigners. By attributing the British defeat to their inability to adapt to wilderness conditions, Cooper defines the limit of paternal authority as the point where changing conditions require an adaptation of the culture.

Though Corny learns to shun dependence at Ticonderoga,

he must himself pass through a crucial adaptation to the unique requirements of the wilderness before becoming truly independent. He is guided by one last surrogate father: the Indian Susquesus. Little older than Corny and his companions, he nevertheless assumes rigorous paternal authority to lead them toward the self-discipline required to conquer the wilderness without being conquered by it. Knowing that unseen enemies have been at work around their bivouac, Susquesus stations Corny in the dark and commands him to listen. For Corny, the vigil is a night journey into the moral darkness of nature and of human nature. Although in Cooper's fiction the young hero experiences evil in the external world rather than in his own soul, the prose takes on a power reminiscent of Hawthorne's explorations of initiation in "Young Goodman Brown" and "My Kinsman, Major Molineux." The American wilderness is no Eden:

> . . . the gloom of the woods being added to the obscurity of the hour, it lent an intensity of blackness to the trunks of the trees, that gave to each a funereal and solemn aspect. It was impossible to see for any distance, and the objects that were visible were only those that were nearest at hand. Notwithstanding, one might imagine the canopied space beneath the tops of the trees, and fancy it, in the majesty of its gloomy vastness. . . . The summits of the giant oaks, maples and pines, formed a sort of upper world as regarded us; a world with which we had little communication, during our sojourn in the woods below. The raven, and the eagle, and the hawk, sailed in that region, above the clouds of leaves beneath them, and occasionally stooped, perhaps, to strike their quarry; but, to all else, it was inaccessible, and to a degree invisible.
>
> But, my present concern is with the world I was in; and what a world it was! Solemn, silent, dark, vast and mysterious. . . . Everything, at that moment, seemed stilled to the silence of death. (376–77)

Since Corny is literally unable to see in the darkness, the world he describes is, for him, an imagined one and, therefore, metaphorically reflects his moral experience as he waits to hear the groans of a tortured man. Led away from even the surveyor's cabin – the most rudimentary outpost of civilization – Corny for the first time comprehends the absolute darkness of the wilderness. Strip the world of civilization and one finds a vast cavern where men move through an "intensity of blackness" and a "stillness so profound" that it takes an extraordinary effort even to imagine any "upper" transcendental world. If there are greater powers operating in this forest, Corny can only imagine them as malevolent. Like the dark omens of an Anglo-Saxon battleground, the raven, the eagle, and the hawk sweep beneath the clouds of leaves only to "strike their quarry." In order to endure the wilderness, as yet "inaccessible, and to a degree invisible," as if forgotten by God, Corny must summon unknown reserves of self-discipline and draw on the example of his Indian mentor. If he responds to the pleas of the tortured man, he will be killed himself and expose those who depend on his protection. He learns that in the wilderness, beyond the restraints of civilization, men need more, rather than less, discipline – that the American must win independence by incorporating the father within the self, rather than by rejecting him.

Having passed through his night journey in the wilderness underworld, Corny, in quick succession, defends his future home at Ravensnest, wins Anneké's hand, and returns to his father's house at Satanstoe. These final episodes, completing his cyclical journey, confirm simultaneously his manhood and his mental transformation from dependent colonist to independent American. The battle at Ravensnest and his marriage secure the future of his family's progress into the new nation's interior; his final return both to his father and to his native place metaphorically suggests that Corny's leaving home by careful stages has allowed as much for the continuity of his family and its values as for his independence.

The small but crucial role of the father now becomes clear. In *The Wept*, the patriarch's dominance of his children and grandchildren was symptomatic of his too abrupt break from the past and the threat that break posed for the future. In *Satanstoe* the father steps back to create a place for his son. As an ideal eighteenth-century parent, he expresses his affection and trust – the keys to his authority – not by constant attention, but by facilitating Corny's independence. He waits at the end of the novel to mark his son's achievement. Because the father has understood it as his duty to oversee the incorporation of his fatherhood by his son, the son reaches maturity without having to rebel against or reject the father. Through a process of gradually reevaluating his surrogate fathers, Corny, on his part, preserves the worthy aspects of his heritage. By returning to his father, Corny fulfills the Lockean assumption that "only by granting such liberty . . . might that new and greater family be made possible, which can only be founded by the free and affectional choice of children to return to the parental roof" (Fliegelman 83). Fliegelman amplifies the point:

> Neither Locke nor Rousseau conceived of the granting of independence to grown children to be synonymous with, or necessarily antecedent to, the dissolution of the family. The point was not so much to create autonomous individuals, as individuals who could and would participate in society. They are made independent so they may become social and ultimately more truly filial. The granting of filial independence permitted the family to reorganize on a voluntaristic, equalitarian, affectional, and, consequently, more permanent basis. (33)

Corny's independent adventures nurture necessary change so that he can bring the colonial past into the American future. His return to Satanstoe shows that his adaptation to unique American conditions does not entail sacrificing the best of the past or of the future. This founder need not jeopardize his offspring. Corny stands ready to assume patriarchal responsibility at the head of the American family, yet, unlike Heathcote, he has forged of himself a link between past and future.

The return to his birthplace further suggests that Corny's independence is rooted rather than uprooting. At the opening of his account, Corny refers to England as "home" and exuberantly identifies the family's farm by its place in the British Empire. His geography draws once again on the comforting image of the individual coddled within concentric spheres:

> I was born on the 3d May, 1737, on a neck of land, called Satanstoe, in the county of West Chester, and in the colony of New York; a part of the widely extended empire that then owned the sway of His Sacred Majesty, George II., King of

Great Britain, Ireland, and France; Defender of the Faith; and,
I may add, the shield and panoply of the Protestant Succession;
God bless him! (10–11)

At the book's end, Corny retains his wonderful capacity for
enthusiasm, but focuses it on his native ground – "I love every
tree, wall, knoll, swell, meadow, and hummock about the old
place" (454). Provincialism and pride in the empire have been
supplanted by love of *patria,* defined literally in Cooper's novel
as the land of one's father. Speaking of George Washington's
post-Revolutionary status as father of the country, Fliegelman
identifies "the kernel of the revolutionary insight [that] the title
of father was transferable" (Fliegelman 197). In *Satanstoe,* Corny
transfers his filial loyalty from the king directly to the land.
Corny's education paves the way for a new definition of loyalty
asserted by his son. After the Revolution, Mordaunt Littlepage
criticizes Tories like his grandfather Herman Mordaunt for remaining "loyal, as it was called; meaning loyalty to a prince,
and not loyalty to the land of their nativity" (*The Chainbearer*
8).

If, as I have argued, the analogy between the development
of an individual and a new nation is central to Cooper's historical
study, then this final insistence on what could fairly be called
the fatherhood of the American landscape is crucial. The nation's
character would be made up of sensations experienced by the
colony – the childhood state of the incipient nation. If the colony
only recognized British elements of its experience, then the colonial past would have already created a culturally dependent
America. Therefore, Corny's warm account of his father's salt-
water farm, and those descriptive set pieces that have most im-
pressed modern readers – sledding through the streets of Albany,
the terrifying breakup of the frozen Hudson, the incomparably
beautiful prospect of Lake George at dawn – must all be understood to work against this anxiety about British domination of
American consciousness. Such experiences, native to the American scene, would constitute a national identity.

In another vein, Anneké reminds Corny to develop a more
independent attitude toward England, not by rejecting the past,
but by acknowledging its diversity. Both his mother and hers

are Dutch; the colony does not owe everything to England. Significantly, she urges this at the moment she accepts his hand, thus promoting the continued intermixture of these cultural elements in America's future. Looking back to the British defeat at Ticonderoga, we can see its function more clearly. Corny's horror at seeing English troops slaughtered not only undermines the main premise of his pro-English surrogate fathers – that English forms and power will dominate in America – but also shocks his order of perception so deeply that new room is given to his American and Dutch experience. The defeat of the British secures his independent perspective, and in terms of Lockean psychology, independent vision secures an independent self.

As the later volumes of *The Littlepage Manuscripts* drew closer to the present, Cooper's tone became more strident. Always acutely aware of his minority position, Cooper despaired of overcoming the public's acceptance of what seemed to him a debased idea of democratic society; he lost confidence in his narrative's ability to re-create readers by manipulating their aesthetic experience. In the Lockean model of education, one sensation made as powerful an impression on the forming consciousness – or, to place the issue on a larger scale, on the forming culture – as the next. Therefore, until an individual's reason was educated, the false rhetoric of Cooper's opponents would be just as influential as careful logic. In fact it would be more so – not because it was right, but because there was more of it. In *The Redskins,* Cooper's constant lashing out against demagoguery, his nit-picking, his harping on incorrect usage, stemmed from a compulsion to educate the public's reason to distinguish the true from the false. Since quantity was more determinant than quality, Cooper wrote as if he had to meet the deluge of public misinformation with an equal measure of correct and corrective information. In part, this courageous, if misguided, sense of struggle against heavy odds explains the Pyrrhic courtroom battles Cooper fought only to win paltry damages and enormous ridicule; these too were the duty of a true democrat (Grossman 6). In print, as in court, his voice sounded a nineteenth-century jeremiad.

In *The Redskins,* the trilogy's final volume, the Littlepage family of the 1840s no longer provides a base from which the young hero can venture out into society. Corny Littlepage's great-grandson retreats into the family circle as a last line of defense. The patriarch's house at Ravensnest, built by Herman Mordaunt to shelter his settlers from Indian attack, now protects the founder's family from the descendants of those very settlers. It has become an armed camp. To Cooper, the isolation of the Littlepage family signaled the final split of contemporary American society from its founding principles. The violence of the Anti-Rent movement fulfilled Cooper's worst anxieties about his country's revolutionary heritage; these latter-day "rebels" had become oppressors (35). In Cooper's hyperbolic rhetoric, the legal changes they proposed were "far more tyrannical than the attempt of Great Britain to tax her colonies, which brought about the revolution" (x).

Yet he was too honest an artist to exclude the negative consequences of this isolation on the founding family itself. Cut off from the easy intercourse between classes characteristic of the earlier stages of society, Hugh Littlepage and his Uncle Ro may no longer claim the representative status of their ancestors. After Corny Littlepage's engaging openness and his affectionate account of *patria,* it comes as a shock, not to mention a literary disappointment, to find Hugh Littlepage a snob whose idea of family genealogy reads more like a real estate audit than a celebration of a family's association with the land. To select but a short sample of his ledger keeping:

> My uncle Ro, however, had got both Satanstoe and Lilacsbush; two country-houses and farms, which, while they did not aspire to the dignity of being estates, were likely to prove more valuable, in the long run, than the broad acres which were intended for the patrimony of the elder brother. My grandfather was affluent; for not only had the fortune of the Littlepages centered in him, but so did that of the Mordaunts, the wealthier of the two, together with some exceedingly liberal bequests from a certain Col. Dirck Follock. . . . my aunts having handsome legacies, in the way of bonds and mortgages, on an estate called Mooseridge, in addition to some lots in town; while my own sister, Martha, had a clear fifty thousand dollars in money. I had town-lots, also, which were becoming

> productive; and a special minority of seven years had made
> an accumulation of cash that was well vested in New York
> State stock, and which promised well for the future. (7–8)

For places that have become associated not only with earlier
narrators but also, by this point in *The Littlepage Manuscripts,*
with the growth of the Republic to be valued primarily as financial assets is a dismaying sign of decline. In a still more as-
tonishing departure from Corny Littlepage's love for "every
tree, wall, knoll, swell, meadow, and hummock" of Satanstoe,
readers are told that Uncle Ro has unceremoniously sold nearly
half of the farm for one hundred ten thousand dollars; he avows
that he made an even greater killing on Lilacsbush: "Ah, *that*
was a clean transaction. . . . I got three hundred and twenty-
five thousand dollars, in hard cash. I would give no credit, and
have every dollar of the money, at this time, in good six per
cent. stock of the States of New York and Ohio" (16). Although
the teller supports the Littlepages' cause, his tale exposes, with
some disgust, that the "greedy rapacity for money" that characterized New York society had wound its way into the patriarch's house.

The besieged family of the patriarch becomes the dominant
image of Cooper's late frontier tales. As early as 1838, Cooper
had written to Horatio Greenough longing to be in Italy with
his friend and lamenting his family's alienation from the people
of Cooperstown:

> There is very little attachment to home, in my family. The
> tastes and habits of the girls are above the country, and they
> take refuge in themselves against ill breeding, coarse flirtations
> and ignorance. They try to love their country, but duty lies
> at the bottom of their effort, and not feeling. They have been
> ill-treated too, and that does not increase the attachment. (3:
> 330)

In these circumstances, he tells his friend, "our family circle is
our world, and has long been so, and everyday I prize it more"
(3: 38). The image of the family as an oasis rather than as the
hub of radiating connections to an integrated society reflects
Cooper's desire to retreat behind the affection and respect of his
family and friends – an impulse that opposed and alternated with

his contentious engagement with American society. That radical alternation characterized Cooper's era. With as little success as Andrew Jackson, who named his plantation the Hermitage in 1804 to signal his hope of bowing from "the stage of public life" and returning "to domestic ease," Cooper resisted his own compulsion to participate in the "circulation, motion, and boiling agitation" of American public life (Rogin 64–65).

Placing the family in opposition to society heralds an important change in Cooper's treatment of the frontier. As his prognosis for American society became more pessimistic and more certain, he lost interest in the frontier as an experimental ground on which to explore the possibilities of American development. The scenario of degeneration had become fixed: the antisocial tendencies inherent in the westward migration triumph over the virtues of leaders like the Littlepages. In the late fiction, particularly in *The Crater* (1847), the experimental aspect of the romance focuses on the frontier as a retreat from society – an idea that he approaches far more sympathetically than he had twenty years before when Heathcote deserted the firesides of his forefathers in *The Wept of Wish-Ton-Wish*.

6

The Patriarch as Isolato:
In Control from Creation to
Apocalypse

The nakedly fantastic plot of *The Crater* reveals more about Cooper's personal stake in the patriarch than any book since *The Pioneers* – that embryonic source of both the Leatherstocking tales and the novels of frontier settlement. In the tradition of exotic sea tales, Cooper, like the ancient mariner, commands the reader to his will, insisting that his narrative is entirely factual. But we are not misled for long, nor are we meant to be. The introduction, falling in tone somewhere between a definition of romance and a refusal to give a refund, prepares us for a bizarre world entirely and self-consciously of Cooper's making. First, he casts his hero on a barren reef; when additional characters demand greater acreage, the author – as First Cause – lifts a new archipelago above the ocean; when his characters anger him, he reaches down and apocalyptically destroys his newly created domain. For Cooper, the Pacific Ocean is a blank slate. On it, he inscribes his major preoccupations as an American artist as clearly as Poe charts the twists of A. Gordon Pym's psyche on the latitudes and longitudes of his South Atlantic. On this watery frontier, where the land cultivated by Cooper's pioneer is so patently land brought forth from the brow of the hero's creator, the connection between Cooper's assessment of patriarchal authority and his own claim to authority as a writer looms before the reader.

Signaling its revealing transparency, the romance begins at the end of its hero's life. Mark Woolston, former patriarch of the lost Pacific paradise, has buried himself for the last forty years in the pastoral anonymity of Bucks County, Pennsylvania. As narrator, Cooper crustily identifies with Mark's retreat from American life. Though Woolston has "strictly acquitted himself of all his public duties," he is rumored to have "regarded all popular demonstrations with distaste, and, as some of his enemies pretended, with contempt" (vii). Cooper's narrative of youth, adventure, and authority springs from an initial image of age and impotence. The story's inverse order reveals the romance's most vital source. Burdened by public rejection and confined within a narrow family circle during the housebound winter of 1847, Cooper projected a fantasy of absolute authority and control.

That fantasy announces itself by an unbroken pattern of wish-fulfillment informing every level of the romance from its preliminary plottings to its close.[1] Returning from his first voyage before the mast, the manly youth is rewarded by the noticeable sexual ripening of his young friend Bridgit Yardley, "bursting into young womanhood" (18). On his second return, the bud has blown into full flower and the scent sweetened by Bridgit's recently acquired fortune, willed to her at the untimely death of her mother. As an unwitting measure of the romance's underpinnings in wish-fulfillment, Mrs. Yardley, falling victim to an editorial lapse, dies twice during the course of the tale – leaving a large fortune on each occasion.

The true action of the narrative begins with an act of filial disobedience – a secret elopement à la Romeo and Juliet. Cooper claims that "much of that which Mark and Bridgit subsequently suffered, was in consequence of acting directly in the face of the wishes and injunctions of their parents," but, in fact, Cooper consistently transforms the prodigal son's punishments into rewards (23).

This pattern begins during the shipwreck that Mark, like his frequently recalled predecessor Robinson Crusoe, "suffers" for his rebellion against paternal authority and the Fifth Commandment. Yet as the first consequence of this horrifying event, Mark's captain is washed overboard, leaving Mark, his first mate, to assume his authority: "A feeling of horror and of regret came over [Mark] at first, but understanding the necessity of self-command, he aroused himself, at once, to his duty, and gave his orders coolly and with judgment" (46). Conveniently, the requirements of the night save Mark from having to examine whether he really feels deep regret at an event that launches him into a position of supreme authority. He embraces his fate with the readiness accorded an act of Providence perfectly attuned to, if not identical with, his own will. Later in the night, the storm carries away the second mate, who had challenged his youthful authority, and all the crew save one perfectly obedient sailor, Bob Betts. As a reference to *The Tempest* makes clear, Cooper's rebel has been awarded the authority of a "king's son" (64). On the morning after his affliction, Mark Woolston and his miraculously unscathed ship of state ride peacefully at anchor beside an extinct crater surrounded by an unnavigable circle of reefs. He gazes at the russet-mantled seascape during "that solemn hour in the morning when objects first grow distinct, ere they are touched with the direct rays from the sun, and when everything appears as if coming to us fresh and renovated from the hands of the Creator" (51). More fortunate than Gatsby and other latter-day Americans, Mark Woolston has the promise of the New World before rather than behind him.

Even the "nakedness" and "dreariness" of the crater to which he has been led "as it might almost be by the hand of Providence," is less a deprivation than a reward (61, 64). It leaves the island a virgin land; after "thousands of years in its nakedness," he now has the power to bring it to "fruitfulness" (104). In fact, its total blankness means that Mark stands before the world, not so much as Adam on the sixth day of creation, as the Creator on the morning of the third, with only sea and land divided. Though he later discovers an overflowing tropical paradise and names it after the original Eden, Cooper's hero never loses his preference for the bare rock on which he's worked his will. On the crater, Mark Woolston enjoys not only the paternal authority against which he had rebelled but also the authority of the first artist and creator. Whether Cooper was consciously punning or not, his fiction persistently elides the two terms – Creator: crater. Like the fictional romance containing it, the crater is self-consciously *made*.

In chronicling Mark's progress, Cooper's prose emphasizes the process of wish-fulfillment and constantly reminds us that

the world before our eyes is fictional. The style differs markedly
from more characteristic adventure writing where credibility
requires suppressing the reader's consciousness of the text and
its author in favor of absolute concentration on the object. Action
writing creates a strong sense of prior reality; the narrative seems
merely to report it. Cooper returns to that more characteristic
mode, for example, when he describes the challenge of bringing
a large ship to anchor underhanded in a small harbor:

> By the time he had [the jib] well in, the ship was off the end
> of the sunken reef, when Bob put his helm a-starbord and
> rounded it. Down came the main-topmast staysail, and Mark
> jumped on the forecastle, while he called out to Bob to lash
> the helm a-lee. In an instant Bob was at the young man's side,
> and both waited for the ship to luff into the wind, and to
> forge as near as possible to the reef. This was successfully
> done also, and Mark let go the stopper within twenty feet of
> the wall of the sunken reef, just as the ship began to drive
> astern. The canvas was rolled up and secured, the cable payed
> out, until the ship lay just mid-channel between the island and
> the sea-wall without, and the whole secured. (73)

While this passage lacks the brilliant, innovative colloquialism
of Dana's similar account in *Two Years Before the Mast* (1840) –
"this picking up of your cables is a very nice piece of work" –
it is a solid example of action writing (111). Together, the para-
tactic linking of short clauses, the frequent shifts between subjects – ship, captain, mate, sail – the preponderance of action
verbs and technical nouns, and the suppression of adjectives
capture the breakneck pace and convince readers that the mar-
iners have no second chance.

   In *The Crater* generally, however, details of remarkable spec-
ificity do not encourage belief in a real crater set in a real ocean;
they seem to refer us instead to a real author's flaunted ability
to satisfy his hero's every need within the imaginary garden of
his fiction. As Franklin observes: "He was describing nothing
here; he was creating" (204). Although "shipwrecked," Mark's
vessel finds a perfectly safe and convenient berth; when the
poultry are thirsty, a shower replenishes their supply; when
hungry, tiny crustaceans fall with the rain – mannah from the
novel's creator. In fact, the problems of setting up house on a

desert island are so consistently overcome that before long we cannot help noticing that difficulties crop up, less as true obstacles, than as opportunities for the hero to display his control over the world.

In *The Crater,* gardening is Cooper's principal metaphor for creativity and there the process of wish-fulfillment sprouts full blown. The lifeless crater floor is, on closer inspection, only a thin crust over a soil so friable it barely needs spading; perfectly composted loam is discovered on a nearby reef – there are no weeds in it; guano deposits abound on neighboring rocks but not on the reef, miraculously tabooed to the useful but evil-smelling cormorant; twice, after Mark sets out his grass seed, a gentle rain falls. Anyone who has killed a plant knows there is no attempt at verisimilitude here.

Nevertheless, the "rapture" Mark feels on finding that his first seeds have taken and flourished is not the joy of an effortless paradise – of freedom from labor (103). Mark and his companion have worked constantly, raising by hand each bucket of soil and compost to the craggy summit of the crater. Rather, his gardening calls into being a promise of merit consistently rewarded. By 1847 it is this fantasy that elicits from Cooper's imagination the fresh, green breast of a new world.

In both speed and luxuriousness, Mark's success frequently recalls Raphael's account of the creation in *Paradise Lost:*

> He scarce had said, when the bare earth, till then
> Desert and bare, unsightly, unadorned,
> Brought forth the tender grass, whose verdure clad
> Her universal face with pleasant green;
> The herbs of every leaf, that sudden flow'red,
> Opening their various colors, and made gay
> Her bosom, smelling sweet: and these scarce blown,
> Forth flourished thick the clust'ring vine, forth crept
> The swelling gourd, up stood the corny reed
> Embattled in her field: And the humble shrub,
> And bush with frizzl'd hair implicit: last
> Rose as in dance the stately trees.
>
> (VII: 313–24)

In Milton's epic, Adam listens passively to Raphael's account of God's previous creation; in *The Crater,* Mark himself brings forth with "prolific humor" the latent fertility of the earth (VII: 280). The speed of the narrative, which in Raphael's plunging lines points to the mystery of divine creation, points in *The Crater* to the writer's ability to create a world of his own making.

Mark's explorations of the surrounding waters deepen the sense of a world projected from the self. In need of fertilizer, the sailors discover a raft of seaweed drifting "directly towards the crater" and then spy a convenient "bay . . . where it may be lodged" (99); in need of an anchorage for a small boat, he finds "a natural basin which was just large enough for such a purpose" (156); later, when Mark is caught on the open ocean close to a lea shore, an opening in the perpendicular rocks appears "just as the sun was setting" – he not only escapes danger, but finds as well "a basin, or bay, of considerable extent" with "a long and wide sandy beach" and a clear, sweet spring (174). Such "discoveries" in the topography of Mark's Reef forge a further Promethean analogy between character and writer, and between writer and Creator. Exercising his control, Cooper chooses to imagine a world where sheltering basins repeatedly open to embrace his hero's needs.

Creating his island gives Mark so much satisfaction that the idea of escape from the avowed misfortune of his shipwreck must be self-consciously resuscitated. Mark barely convinces himself; to readers it is already obvious that the crater itself represents escape from any authority in conflict with his own. He soon modifies his plan; he will leave only long enough to retrieve his young wife and return to live "in the midst of its peace and tranquility" (120). When he senses a "feeling of regret" even at the prospect of that mission, Cooper saves him the trouble by washing away his only means of escape and his sole companion.

It is a measure of Cooper's desire for uncontested sway that his hero enjoys his deepest satisfactions during the period of absolute isolation following this calamity. In that solitude, Cooper translates the traditional virtues of monastic retreat into the terms of his South Sea romance: "Cut off, as he was, from all communion with his kind, . . . Mark found himself, *by a very natural operation of causes,* in much closer communion with his Creator, than he might have been in the haunts of the world" (141; emphasis added). In a novel so self-consciously fantastic, "natural" causes are always suspect. By ascribing the terminology of voluntary religious retreat to the ostensibly involuntary retreat of his adventurer, Cooper serves notice that acts of God – turns of plot – that leave Mark Woolston alone satisfy his hero's volition as precisely as the natural basin satisfies his ship's need for shelter.

Mark's "closer communion with his Creator" proceeds with a purgative lesson in humility. A fever leaves him "unconscious of even his own existence, in a state as near death as life" while "everything possessing life [in his garden creation] had actually been living in abundance" (138). Yet, oddly, this *memento mori* leads him less to human abasement than to communion with God's divine power. Awaking from his fever, Mark sees before him a miniature version of the created world. Like Peale's museum or Rittenhouse's orrery – still more like Bartram's botanical garden – his island, scarce wanting "any plant that was then known to the kitchens of America" (107), allows him to see more clearly God's rational order and becomes the focus of his Deistic worship. To Mark, as to other Americans of his period, "the sight of God at work in his creation" comes to be "experienced as more powerful than his immediate presence in his word" (Fliegelman 213). But as Jefferson's extravagant praise of Rittenhouse's machine implied, worlds-in-little call attention not only to God's rational plan – to God as Enlightenment man – but also to Enlightenment man as god – to the genius of the human diviner and his capacity to reproduce God's creation so as to claim a share in God's authorship.

By referring to God as the "Author of [human] happiness," influential Deistic texts, like Webster's 1831 "Speller," allied divine creativity specifically to the creativity of the writer. When Mark struggles from his sick bed, he learns he has created a world that lives beyond him as a romance lives beyond its author. As a passive invalid, he experiences the divine nature of his own creativity. When his island world gives him comfort and solace, he enjoys filial dependence on his own fatherhood. He is a reader of his own book. Cooper thus collapses God, writer, and character.

Mark Woolston's worship takes a second classic Deist form in his "healthful communion with the stars" (141). Aided by "a very neat reflecting telescope," he rationally contemplates the power behind the universe:

> Hours at a time did Mark linger on the Summit, . . . his spirit struggling the while to get into closer communion with that dread Being which had produced all these mighty results; among which the existence of the earth, its revolutions, its heats and colds, its misery and happiness, are but specks in the incidents of a universe. (143)

His study rewards him with a better understanding of "his own position in the scale of created beings" (143). Again, this is only partially a lesson in humility. A secure place in the great chain of created beings not only banishes feelings of alienation and displacement, it gives the right and duty to exert patriarchal control over the rest of creation. Thus, Mark's next order of business is to make "a regular survey of all his possessions, inquiring into the state of each plant he had put into the ground, as well as into that of the ground itself" (145).

Within Cooper's romance, Mark Woolston's surveys become a sub-genre charting the circumference of the patriarch's control. Like Jefferson, in *Notes on the State of Virginia*, Cooper's hero attends to the most minute botanical and geological details. He studies "oranges, lemons, cocoa-nuts, limes, figs . . . melons, of both sorts, the tomatoes, the egg-plants, the peppers, cucumbers, onions, beans, corn, sweet-potatoes" – here we are within a decade of Whitman and Thoreau (145). In the second and colonial half of the romance, his expanded survey includes the encyclopedic categories of Jefferson's original *Notes:* there is a census, a summary of the archipelago's political institutions, a geography, a catalogue of resources and industries, a classification of its flora, fauna, and fish. Made during two monarchlike passages through his augmented realm, they chart the rise and fall of his patriarchy.

Mark Woolston's surveys enact the distinguishing Enlightenment strategy of asserting control over the world by sending out the rational mind to measure, classify, and comprehend it. Jefferson wrote *Notes on the State of Virginia* mainly during a rare period of retreat from public life (Peden xi). From the confines of his small study, Jefferson took possession of his state.

At Monticello as at Concord, one is surprised by the small studies reduced to the essential light of fire, bookcase, desk, chair,
and pen; within these nutshells Jefferson and Emerson counted
themselves kings of American space. Jefferson sent out his reason, not merely to scout and spy in Hobbesian fashion, but to
survey and claim. By this strategy he prepared to reassert his
political authority. Later in his career he sent Lewis and Clark
out from Washington to extend America's authority over the
West and the future.

In similar fashion, Mark Woolston surveys "his possessions"
to commune with the *power* of "that dread Being which has
produced all these mighty results." When he looks down from
his summit, rather than up to the stars, he sees mighty results
of his own making. Though his horticultural catalogues owe
most to the Enlightenment, they also possess the world, as
Whitman's catalogues do, by a Romantic expansion of the ego
into the world. Mark Woolston's song is the created world of
the crater.

That *The Crater* looks back to Jefferson and forward to Whitman illustrates how fully the Enlightenment's preoccupation
with natural sciences informs American Romanticism. But,
more crucially, the seemingly bizarre association of Cooper's
strategies with Whitman's exposes the fragility of Mark Woolston's extravagant claims of union and control. Whitman's assertion of identity with the world's profuse variety plants seeds
of doubt within his hearers, and within the singer himself, that
start up like dragon's teeth to challenge the reality of his vision.
This process gives both "Song of Myself" and *Leaves of Grass*
their rhythm of flowing assertion and halting doubt. By contrast,
the very perfection of Mark's solitary control alerts readers to
his world's artificiality. The more minutely Cooper explains
the natural world of the crater, the more self-consciously artificial it seems. Though celebrating the writer's power to create
and control a world of words, the first half of the romance also
underscores the limitations of that power.

Both the power and the implicit frustrations of the isolato's retreat give birth to the vast archipelago Mark colonizes in the
romance's second half. On the one hand, the sea-change, decked

out with language evocative of Genesis, flaunts the writer's power to play God with defiant exuberance. At Cooper's command, an earthquake "thrust upward a vast surface of the reef, completely altering the whole appearance of the shoal! In a word, nature [read, art] had made another effort, and the islands had been created, as it might be in the twinkling of an eye" (162). Climbing his new "discovery," Cooper's hero sweeps the horizon with his glass. From this God-like elevation he sees his expanded "possessions" "truly resembling a vast dark-looking map, spread upon the face of the waters for his special examination" (187, 186). On the other hand, the return to the scenario of frontier settlement presaged by this territorial expansion reflects Cooper's temperamental inability to accept those limits on the artist's authority implicit in the obvious artificiality and in the isolation of Mark Woolston's retreat. Seen in this light, The Crater's two-part structure, with its return to the issues of governing a republic, is an attempt to extend the control achieved in retreat out into society. The fantasy of retreat becomes the fantasy of perfect patriarchal control and tests whether the control achieved in the suspended time of Mark's solitude can survive in the real time of sexual generation and family.

In Cooper's life, the urge to move from domestic retreat to public engagement constituted a dominant theme of his correspondence and emerged with particular clarity while he was writing The Crater, in the winter, spring, and summer of 1847. The winter was hard; Cooper reported being cut off by an awful tempest in March – "For days we had no mail" (5: 207); three feet of snow still lay on the ground early in April; a 10-degree frost struck on April 16. "Mrs. Cooper's indisposition has kept me at home," he wrote, and he felt the longing of the "wearied worldling" he describes in The Crater, "who sighed for the enjoyment of his old haunts, after a season passed in the ennui of his country house" (5: 206; 176).

During this confinement, the striking feature of his correspondence is a series of long letters about the Mexican War to his friend from his days of naval service William Bradford Shubrick.[2] In exchanges detailing both the military and political plottings of the Mexican campaign, Cooper vicariously participated in the leading events of his day. Shubrick commanded the Pacific fleet; Cooper commanded Shubrick. The novelist's rolling epistolary style bound together threads of naval gossip, descriptions of the debated islands and straits of the Northwest border, newspaper accounts of Mexican land campaigns plagued by yellow fever, disdain for Matthew Perry's bravado, astute assessments of European interests, the relative merits of blockade or siege. Most revealing was the note of jealousy he showed toward his fellow historian George Bancroft (V: 118–19). Bancroft had successfully translated his authority as writer of the *History of the United States* into direct executive authority as Polk's secretary of the navy. Although cordial friends, the position of the younger man must have been a bitter draught for the author of *The History of the Navy of the United States of America* (1839). Under the pressure of his isolation, Cooper's desire to engage in public affairs spills over into the second half of *The Crater*.

The enlargement of *The Crater*'s scale changes Mark Woolston's mode of action and even his motives. The impulse to survey his surroundings takes on the flavor of the bustling expansionism of mid-century America. Despite Cooper's bitter denunciations of this spirit in novel after novel, his fantasy lives and breathes it. From the summit of the crater, "his limits were so much enlarged as to offer something like a new world to his enterprise and curiosity" (163). With "enterprise" added to the vocabulary of "new world" promise, Mark's discoveries, even his gardening, take on an imperial dimension. Where Mark once stumbled on sea-weed deposits suitable for asparagus beds, he now looks over a vast plain and names it "the Prairie" (178); where he chanced on a perfect refuge for his dinghy, he now sails into wide harbors drawn to the scale of Cole's more fantastical landscapes, with natural jetties marked by lighthouselike columns of rock. Cooper hails "our explorer" and compares him, no longer to Robinson Crusoe, but to Columbus (182). Exploration soon leads to acquisition: a fleet of whaling ships swells the colony's coffers; a small navy gives Mark "complete command of the adjacent seas" (257). Taking up the idolatrous sandalwood trade, Woolston extends his sway westward along the course of empire to China. In his new guise, Mark commands a changed Pacific frontier. Once a sanctuary, it now takes on the dominant cultural associations of the mid-century frontier: it is a "mine of wealth" (298).

With this shift in emphasis from creation to acquisition, Cooper's metaphors evoke correspondingly changed ideas of art. At the point of the crater's transformation from retreat to territory, Cooper introduces the famous analogy between the rise and fall of his Pacific kingdom and Cole's magnificent series of paintings "The Course of Empire." Sailing toward the dark column of smoke hanging over the earth-altering volcano, Mark Woolston spies a new island, "The Peak," "a sublime sight, issuing, as it did, from the ocean without any relief . . . in all its glory, blue and misty, but ragged and noble" (176). Like Cole's craggy summit, the fixed point around which his five canvases turn, Cooper's newly created Peak and its ominous column of smoke will serve as "eternal land-marks" to betoken the fate of the colony (172). As a retreat, the crater needed no such eternal sign; on it, Mark Woolston achieved an ahistorical stasis – deeply connected with natural cycles of growth, decay, and replenishment, but free of dynastic cycles of rise and fall.

In the romance's first half, art allies itself, not with mimesis or synthetic recombination, but with God-like creation from the void. In the second half, Mark's sense of art moves from the Biblical to the imperial. When a new world swims into Mark's ken – like Keats, Cooper links his explorer to Herschel – he contemplates it and then, like Adam Verver, possesses it: after "gazing at this height with as much pleasure as the connoisseur ever studied picture, or statue, the young man determined to attempt a voyage to that place" (176). Just as the activities of writer and hero are closely bound in *The Crater*'s first half, so in the second Cooper's writing, instead of dedicating itself to the evocation of an ideal world, more aggressively asserts its claim to authority over the world as found.

Soon after Mark explores his new territory, a search party led by Bob Betts, Mark's wife, his sister, and his brother-in-law finds Mark and establishes a colony of select immigrants under his stewardship. In the early stages, Mark achieves satisfaction in the social realm equivalent to the yielding natural world of the crater. In fact, the colony glosses the earlier fantasy of hard work rewarded. Indicatively slipping into the first person, Cooper explains, "In our island community, most of its citizens were accustomed to think that education and practice gave a man certain claims to control" (224). The key term behind authority here, as before, is control. To achieve, in society, the equivalent control he enjoyed as an isolato, Cooper's hero is "unanimously chosen governor for life." His "title and authority to rule" rest on the "special gift of Providence to himself," and the series of steps by which that gift evolves into authority transparently parallels Cooper's aspirations as a writer. As Mark makes of his gift a new world on the barren crater, so Cooper uses his given talents to build a fictional world in his romances. In the second half of *The Crater,* Mark is rewarded, as Cooper hoped to be, with substantial property – the gift incarnate – that, in turn, bestows the mantle of unchallenged social authority; Mark Woolston has, for a moment, "no rival" (327). Twice in his career, Cooper christened his American Abraham with the name Mark – the one who writes and leaves his sign.

Most critics have taken Cooper's introduction of a "charming little colony" as a return to more recognizable frontier reality (5: 215). Cooper fosters the illusion by rehearsing Jeffersonian debates about restrained expansion and by exporting to the Pacific his familiar scenario of frontier decline: the fall from the benevolent order of Woolston's patriarchy to the chaos of a society divided by the four horsemen of Cooper's democracy: lawyer, editor, dissenting minister, and passive citizen. But, in fact, Cooper's own despair of asserting patriarchal authority over mid-century society undermines the familiar "reality" of the romance's second half. Though parallel to his treatment of the American frontier, the history of "governor" Woolston is more accurately seen as a fantasy within the fantasy of retreat.

We celebrate the first half of *The Crater* in its imaginative integrity even if we know its world isn't ours. But despite its catalogues of encyclopedic detail, the second half of the romance gradually unhinges from any sense of an integrated order and so exposes the disjunctive link between the harmonious world of the first half and the violence and disruption of the second, between the isolato's meticulous care and the patriarch's power, between the creative and aggressive impulses of a writer.

From the outset, the fantasy of control over society seems

more remote than the fantasy of retreat. After such perfect isolation, Mark himself has difficulty, Cooper notes, comprehending the reality of his new associates. The isolated paradise
lost seems more real than the community regained:

> It was a long time, notwithstanding, before he could become
> accustomed to the idea of having associates, at all. Time and
> again, within the next month or two, did he *dream* that all
> this fancied happiness was only a *dream,* and awoke under a
> sense of having been the subject of an agreeable illusion. (201)

For readers, the dreamlike quality of these newly introduced
characters persists. Though they inhabit Mark's islands, we do
not hear them in direct discourse. Motives imputed to them
either correspond exactly to the patriarch's will or exactly oppose
it; differentiated mainly by class, they are chess pieces allowing
Mark to extend the play of his imagination over the larger board
of his colony. As such, they encourage readers to see the frontier
scenario as a game rather than as a return to a paradigmatic
investigation of American development.

During the last decade of his life, Cooper lived on a remarkably energetic, high-spirited, and courageous plane, but there
also stirred bitter feelings of rejection. The frontier scenario in
The Crater's second half taps this level of his psyche; suspicion
and wild assertions of power, both symptomatic of his disappointment, direct the narrative.

At times the unconscious consequences play themselves out
in ludicrous juxtapositions and inconsistencies. So tender is
Cooper's sense of control that even his tribute to man's innate
hatred of tyranny must be interrupted with an entirely inap-
plicable caveat: "but it is necessary to distinguish between real
oppression and those restraints which are wholesome, if not
indispensable to human happiness" (254). Although Cooper repeatedly insists that Mark Woolston prefers "happiness to wealth
and morals to power," readers notice that Cooper – whose letters
account for every dollar painfully secured in the face of declining
popularity – inevitably rewards his hero's generous avowals with
the receipt of both wealth and power (297). Mark voices his
preference for happiness and morals shortly after his election as
governor for life and the arrival of an 11,000-dollar award from

an insurance company – for honesty. Cooper warns that prosperity threatens to make the people idle and contentious, but a
paragraph earlier he explains Mark's 100,000-dollar investment
in American six per cents without comment (429–30).

Cooper's treatment of race most clearly reveals his anxieties
about extending his authority, or, reduced to more traumatic
terms, about retaining control over his life when exposed outside
his retreat. Though tenuously traceable to earlier Cooper Indians
or the South Sea islanders of *Typee* (1846), the natives of Cooper's Pacific frontier – led by Ooroony, the smiling and good,
and Waally, the evil of inscrutable face – derive their true literary
ancestry from the phantasmagoric projections of Arthur Gordon
Pym. Cooper's narrative sometimes projects the casual racist
assumptions accompanying his descriptions of blacks in *Satanstoe*
and other novels – "Unus was intelligent for a savage" – and
cavalierly lists "two Kannakas drowned" in the manner of
Huck's synopsis of the steamboat accident – "No'm. Killed a
nigger." But it would be a mistake to dismiss the regressive
childishness of the romance's racism without investigating the
psychological complexity informing Cooper's account.

As he was writing *The Crater,* Cooper acutely perceived how
Americans had capitalized on Mexican weakness to puff up their
self-importance: "Glory is not easily obtained in these Vera
Cruzan Buena Vistan times. No man is glorious that has not
scalped and eaten a Mexican" (5: 211). Within the novel, he
comments on the exploitative nature of free trade with unde-
veloped countries – it gives "the lion's share of the profit to
them who need it least" – and, like Melville, directly attacks
the French and English for their destructive conquests of islanders in Tahiti and New Zealand (97). Yet in his narrative
Cooper sends his hero through a series of analogous supremacist
adventures. Cooper's use of native islanders proceeds from a
compulsion deeper than his conscious disdain for such exploitation. But the parallels between Mark Woolston's juvenile adventures and American intervention against weaker, darker
peoples – intimations of Norman Mailer's *Why are we in Vietnam?*
– warn against dismissing Cooper's compulsion as a merely
personal neurosis; in his fantasy, Cooper is all too representative
an American.

Cooper's native islanders exist chiefly to justify Mark Woolston's desire for power. Though avowedly reluctant to leave the domestic paradise he now inhabits with his wife, Mark rationalizes his return to active command by noting his fear of "foreign invasion" (218). Yet the motives he imputes to "men like the natives" – the passion "to explore" and "to possess" – are precisely the motives of "our explorer" and "governor," owner of more than half the colony (219). His fears of invasion project his own desire for power out into the world, where they are embodied in two-dimensional savages. The effort to deny the aggressive aspect of his self places a premium on treating the savages as other. He randomly labels the same group of islanders as natives, savages, Kannakas, blacks, and Indians, but always in cartoon racist terms. By projecting the *motives* of power onto something external, Mark frees himself to use power laundered of its aggressive and negative connotations: "Our governor had no relish for power for power's sake, but only wielded it for the general good" (326). (The emphatic repetition betrays the true focus of the sentence.) His projected fears of hostility sanctify his own desire for power.

Primitive enemies offer a second advantage. Though Mark faces increasing opposition to his authority within the colony, his dark neighbors furnish an external social world as compliant as the natural world of his retreat. On the stage of an exotic opera buffa, Mark's "natural" claim to authority receives its due recognition and reward; where twelve white men and a small vessel with three guns can control "a people who counted their hosts in thousands," here at last " 'knowledge is power' " (284).

To exercise more fully his authority over foreign affairs, Mark installs a right-thinking new leader at the head of the native government; the new leader immediately contracts to supply the white government with labor and a monopoly on sandalwood, the islands' natural resource, in exchange for "articles of little or no value" (285). The parallels to later American efforts to "change a dynasty" narrow the gap of the last one hundred years (284). To exercise more fully his domestic authority, Mark imports savages to his colony, creating an uncontentious servant class. Though Cooper credits "Mark's good management" with making these "lads" brought up in public service "work and be happy" and refers to them as a "sort of Irish for his colony," he can't successfully hide from his readers that the "sort of Irish" he's describing are slaves. Here are social inferiors who know their place. Later in the romance, when his authority is challenged from within and without the colony, Mark begins to suspect even the most loyal natives. The connection to slavery rears to the surface and Woolston's precautions mimic mid-century fears of slave rebellion. The lack of any visible sign of change in the natives' loyalty causes him only anxiety. As pirates advance, he rounds up and deports the Kannaka field hands, excepting only those most closely attached to his naval service, the colony's equivalent of trusted house servants.

The use of natives as a palliative to patriarchal impotence descends to more open lust for power in Cooper's accounts of Mark's military operations. Although these reflect Cooper's experience as a naval historian, they more directly spring from his vicarious involvement in United States policy. From his isolation in Cooperstown, he advised Shubrick, "In the event of a Mexican war, I should think a great many small vessels would be useful – schooners and brigs, with a few heavy guns, and small crews, so as to float light and sail fast" (5: 52); in *The Crater* he commands just such a fleet. In his relish for power, Cooper exploits the natives with increasing violence and absurdity. Mark Woolston scares away an entire fleet with the noise of his cannon; the savages throw themselves into a suicidal attack so that Mark can feel the satisfaction of watching his grapeshot fly "through the thickest of the assailants" (277); later, Mark rakes the deck of an enemy ship and dispatches "half a dozen" (308); besieged by eleven hundred savages, Cooper's hero stops the attack by killing the top man on a human totem pole with a "bullet in his brains" and by slaughtering a dozen more at the woodpile; the war comes to an end when "a human body, which was cast a great distance in the air, . . . fell, like a heavy clod, across the gunwale of the sloop. This proved to be the body of Waally [leader of the bad], one of the arms having been cut away by a shot, three hours before!" (427).

To readers it becomes dispiritingly evident that Cooper's patriarch takes as much satisfaction in the elaborate planning of military fortifications as he did in the loving cultivation of his garden retreat. The satisfactions seem shockingly parallel. Whereas he carved out cavities in the crater to fill with wheel-barrows of compost, he now chisels batteries into the cliffs of the Peak and implants them with guns (223). Whereas he once rejoiced to discover packets of seed in the ship's cargo, a full paragraph now catalogues the contents of his ship's magazine. Plowshares are beaten into swords.

Creativity and aggression normally stand in opposition, but the two halves of Cooper's romance confront a common impulse behind them. If Mark Woolston's latter-day satisfaction comes not so much from indulging in pure violence as from the sense of power that the natives' weakness and ignorance bestow, it becomes clear that the building of his garden world and his aggression against the "savages" both give him a sense of se-curity and control. When threatened by emptiness – by the void represented by the crater's original barrenness – Mark achieved control and security by creating a world out of nothing. When threatened by conflict and competition – represented by an in-creasingly rebellious colony – he secures control aggressively. Although cultivating gardens and building batteries are not the same, both provide satisfaction to Mark Woolston and to his creator as strategies to preserve the self.

Metaphorically, Cooper seals this connection when he trans-forms the crater from a Deistic oasis into an "impregnable" for-tress (223). Both isolated retreat and aggressively asserted social authority save the self from the governing fear of "invasion." But in the fictions they inform, the linked strategies have widely divergent consequences. Moving from the first half of *The Crater* to the second, readers meet a diminished art, just as they do in moving from Cooper's best passages of mythopoetic description to the aggressively didactic sections of his work. In the second half of the novel Mark Woolston takes the reef he had made into a sign of God's universe and reduces it to a "citadel" that loses its power to signify anything beyond the self's insecurity (265).

The end of the war against the savages brings the sudden

collapse of Mark's authority within the colony, as if the fantasy of unlimited power supported by the savages only held off the inevitable failure of any attempt to extend control from retreat to society. The romance's last pages become abruptly bitter. When the colony proves itself not an extension of the patriarch's self but obdurately "other," Mark denounces his Pacific frontier and it renounces him. By restricting his associations to members of his own class, the patriarch increasingly isolates himself from the rapidly growing colony as later generations of Littlepages isolated themselves from the mid-century America of *The Redskins*. Thus Mark's desire to command society – to extend his will outward from the sheltered circumference of his crater retreat – turns itself around into an assertion of his right to live within the perfect and superior circle of "his own family." From *The Wept,* to *Satanstoe,* to *The Crater,* that circle noticeably shrinks: the fireside gatherings of the entire Puritan community become the more intimate hearthside meetings of the Littlepage family; and punch drinking among family and friends of three generations gives way to rare glimpses of Mark with his "little family"; we see them walking still further turned into each other – "Young Mark held by his mother's hand, while the father led his little daughter . . . probably appearing to each parent that the child thus led was a miniature image of the other" (386–87). Such intimacy might not restrict the easy movement from private to public life in times of crisis, when the example of Cincinnatus called out to Mark Woolston, or Corny Littlepage, or George Washington. But in periods of fat commercial prosperity, enjoyed alike by Mark's colony and Cooper's New York in the decades after the opening of the Erie Canal, retirement becomes withdrawal and signals the loss of authority.

With vengeance, the familial rhetoric of the opening returns in the closing pages of the romance. As Mark's filial rebellion was once rewarded with authority, so his authority is now rewarded with filial rebellion: "To his surprise, as well as to his grief, Pennock [a previously steady subordinate] was seduced by ambition, and he assumed the functions of the executive with quite as little visible hesitation, as the heir apparent succeeds to his father's crown" (443). In Mark and the remaining members of the original leadership, this usurpation induces a nostalgic longing to return to the "land of their fathers before they died" (447). The rebellion of his own followers induces an identification with the father against whom Cooper's prodigal originally rebelled.

When Mark decides to return to America, the people bring suit against him, claiming possession of the crater; and Cooper reiterates a now formulaic account of the controversy with his neighbors over Three-Mile Point.[3] For a late work, *The Crater* is remarkably free of such direct autobiographical intrusion. Mark's creation of a harmonious world at the crater and his efforts to colonize the expanded group functioned so satisfactorily as metaphors that they freed Cooper from his need to intrude didactically into the narrative. The final, sudden return to the more characteristic pattern of his late career signals his despair of fiction's ability to create an alternative world.

After carrying his family to America, Mark returns to the crater to make one last claim to his full authority. In a reversal of his original voyage, he sails as a father in search of his prodigal son. On a conscious level, he turns his face in love toward the wayward colony: "His heart was still in the colony, over the weakness of which his spirit yearned, as the indulgent parent feels for the failings of a backsliding child" (453). But when he arrives where the colony had been, his unconscious will as a punishing father has been done. The "internal fires" of paternal wrath "had wrought a new convulsion, and . . . this time it was to destroy, instead of to create"; his "paradise had sunk beneath the ocean!" (455–56). Finding in the Pacific nothing "to buoy out a lost community," Mark sails back to America to bury himself in the isolation of his rural retirement (458). From that isolation the romance was born.

In the final paragraph, Cooper comes forward to advise humility before the Creator. From a man still vigorous but conscious always of his mortality, the advice no doubt intends what it says: Let the "masses" remember that

> . . . their boasted countries, with their vaunted climates and productions, have temporary possessions of but small portions of a globe that floats, a point, in space, following the course pointed out by an invisible finger, and which will one day be

suddenly struck out of its orbit, as it was originally put there, by the hand that made it. (459)

Coming from an author who two pages earlier had struck a world out of existence, the particular imagery of Cooper's sermon suggests that his caution against "those who would substitute the voice of the created for that of the Creator" implies, at some deeper level, the contrary regret that the writer could not substitute the created world of the crater for the world left to him by his Creator.

Cooper's account of colonization in the romance's second half reflects his continuing desire to wield the political and social power of men like Jay and Jefferson, whose writing accorded them the status of founders. But Cooper discovered that outside those rare moments of crisis that call Cincinnatus to abandon his plow and serve the republic, writer and politician are intractably distinct categories. Despite unrelenting efforts, Cooper could not manufacture a national debacle out of a modest regional upheaval like the antirent disputes. In *Satanstoe,* he made that same region an effective ground for a drama of the nation's evolving independent consciousness, but as he approached his own time and place, he felt the constraints of his position in a small and unpopular minority – an isolation exaggerated by his residence at Cooperstown. Without confidence in his audience, he worried that his fiction would not persuade and slipped into an ineffective rhetorical mode. In a novel like *The Redskins,* he not only lost the advantage of manipulating his readers to his side – there was no longer any real fictional vision for them to share – but also failed in his more direct appeal by placing his political rhetoric in a context where it was bound to disappoint the expectations of even those readers disposed to agree with him. Aware of the ruinous literary consequences but unwilling to pull back, Cooper became still more frustrated, and his tone rose toward belligerence.

The Crater avoids the rhetorical quagmire of *The Redskins.* The opening half of the romance embraces readers within the encircling Pacific reefs with seductive loveliness. Even in the last pages, when the distinctive shapes of Cooper's personal concerns break toward the surface of the narrative, the illusion of Mark Woolston's Pacific kingdom is not entirely lost. Nor would it be correct to attribute *The Crater*'s problems to any more general creative and personal decline. Until the wearing sickness of his last year, Cooper lived and produced with exemplary energy; *The Deerslayer* and *Satanstoe,* among his best romances, are products of his last decade. Ironically, it was Cooper's admirable desire to return to direct engagement with the problems of American politics and society that brought on *The Crater*'s decline as a work of fiction. In this sense, *The Crater* enacts the central problem of his later career. When Cooper's longing for control found a creative channel in the first half of the tale, he succeeded in evoking not only the lovely garden world of the crater but a persuasive vision of a man's reverence and gratitude for the power of creativity bestowed on him. But when that impulse to control directed itself toward recalcitrant political issues, Cooper found it increasingly difficult to overcome the obstacles of his isolation. The problem did not reside so much in the issues themselves – we have surveyed precisely those fictions that successfully embodied them – as in Cooper's difficulty in developing strategies for bringing a problematic world under artistic control.

Despite the problems of *The Crater*'s second half, it is more appropriate to celebrate Cooper's effort to return to a synecdochic treatment of American political and social life than to decry too loudly its failures. Although imagining his hero's solitary life on the crater yielded great satisfaction, Cooper resisted his own idealization of isolation. The first half of *The Crater,* like the Leatherstocking tales, relishes escape from society, but it does little to answer the question of how such individual liberty can be preserved and perpetuated in the social world where, in fact, we have to live. The return to the scenario of frontier settlement marks Cooper's determination not only to ask, "What is an American?" but to demand as well, "What is American society?"

The course of the American Abraham through our literature presents a history of that latter question. Even writers known for their Adamic solitaries turn to the patriarch and the possibilities of the frontier when they want to ask questions of

American society. In his first novel, Mark Twain transformed the story of his father's delusionary westering into the comic legend informing the gilded age; Frank Norris exposed the connections between Magnus Derrick's patriarchal fantasy and the power of the corporate octopus that overwhelmed him; to comprehend the failure of her country's communal values, Willa Cather looked to the seeming disjunction between patriarchal figures like Jim Burden's grandfather or Captain Forrester and the village culture of Wick Cutter and Ivy Peters; John Steinbeck studied the breakdown of the Joads' vestigial frontier patriarchy to analyze the social disintegration he had witnessed in Oklahoma and California.

Preeminently, the tradition descended to William Faulkner. Faulkner's historical imagination, like Cooper's, described his world by narrating the complications of the patriarchal family. History lay in the legacy left by the first Compsons, Sartorises, McCaslins, and de Spains, in the creation of Sutpen's Hundred, in the spreading Snopesian progeny of "Father Abraham." The parallels between Cooper and Faulkner are as extraordinary as the stylistic advances that separated their literary eras. They were alike preoccupied with the dominant male figures of their family histories; they treated the frontier, on the one hand, as an escape from the world and, on the other, as the stage where passion and will enacted the creation of communities out of muddy earth; they alternately projected figures corresponding to those opposed visions of the frontier – solitaries like Natty Bumppo and Ike McCaslin, who were guides to a country and fathers to no one – and patriarchs like Heathcote and Sutpen, designers of their own errands into the wilderness; they habitually assessed the patriarch by his break with the past and its cost to the future – to the children of Ishmael, to Roth McCaslin, to Henry, Judith, and Charles Bon. The triumphs of Faulkner's career and the tradition of the frontier patriarch that descends from Cooper through Nathaniel Hawthorne, Mark Twain, Hamlin Garland, Frank Norris, Ole Rölvaag, Willa Cather, and John Steinbeck demonstrate the continuing place of the patriarchal founder in the American imagination. The American Adam and the American Abraham rotate like twin stars at the center of our literary consciousness.

Notes

Introduction

1 In one of *Moby-Dick*'s best-known passages, Melville exuberantly coins the term *Isolato* to mark the isolated condition of his representative Americans: "How it is, there is no telling, but Islanders seem to make the best whalemen. They were nearly all Islanders in the Pequod, *Isolatoes* too, I call such, not acknowledging the common continent of men, but each *Isolato* living on a separate continent of his own. Yet now, federated along one keel, what a set these Isolatoes were!" (in Chapter 27, "Knights and Squires").

2 Stephen Railton argues that Cooper's "literary career as a whole quintessentially represented his imaginative effort to delineate himself: to assert or achieve his own identity" (33). I share his belief in the importance of Cooper's relationship with his father, but where he, in his quite strict Freudianism, follows the novels back to Cooper's childhood, I give more emphasis to Cooper's successful strategies for gaining authority as an adult.

3 It is probably worth noting the obvious point that in Cooper's time the word "patriarchal" distinguished a particular cluster of political and social relationships in a world that generally assumed male dominance. It had not yet been broadened to its contemporary popular usage as a general term of condemnation for anything pertaining to male-dominated societies.

4 See Forgie, Rogin, and especially Fliegelman's account of Mather's *Magnalia* and of Locke's educational theories.

5 See George Dekker, *James Fenimore Cooper: The American Scott*.

6 Though less well known than the easily anthologized chapter "What Is an American?," the central chapters of the *Letters* use the success of Europeans on the isolated and barren island of Nantucket as a synecdochic study of American principles much as Cooper uses isolated frontier settlements; "What has happened here," Crèvecoeur claimed, "will happen everywhere else" (91).

7 Unless otherwise noted, all quotations of Cooper's fiction are taken from *Cooper's Works*, The New Edition (New York: Stringer & Townsend, 1857).

Chapter 1: Paradigmatic Tensions

1 At the request of his government, François Marbois, the secretary of the French legation at Philadelphia, sent out the questionnaire that Jefferson answered. William Peden notes the suggestion of Gilbert Chinard that Buffon originally framed the questionnaire (*Notes* xii). The intellectual relationship between France and America was intimate. Cooper and Marbois became friends and visited often from 1826 to 1833, when Cooper was living in Europe.

In "To Crispin O'Conner, A Back-Woodsman," Philip Freneau cast Buffon's aspersion back on Europe "where mother-country acts the step-dame's part" (3: 74; Kolodny 9).

2 Phrases in parentheses appear in the British edition of *The Wept* (London, 1833), p. 5. Cooper originally printed *The Wept* in Italy. Workmen unfamiliar with English made many errors. In 1833, Cooper corrected them and made minor clarifications in the text like the one cited here. The text of the New Edition of 1857 was based on the uncorrected American edition of 1829.

3 Although Tocqueville did not publish "A Fortnight into the Wilderness" during his lifetime, he brought these three key pages into the *Democracy*.

Chapter 2: Family Origins and Patriarchal Designs

1 Susan Fenimore Cooper, *Small Family Memories* 38; hereafter cited in the text as SC.

2 Railton sets the two challenges in the context of Cooper's oedipal quest for his mother's affection and approval (70–72).

3 In Cooper's own telling of the tale in the 1849 preface, he multiplies the number of challenges. To the original challenge of a friend he adds a series of discouraging responses from readers of early drafts, which he then felt impelled to overcome (*The Pilot* 1883 vii–x).

4 Wayne Franklin traces Cooper's "sustaining inner drive" to the "forced maturing" brought on by financial difficulties during the 1809–19 period; he too sees Cooper's writing as an effort "to seize control of his life." I link the events of these years more specifically to his development of the patriarchal paradigm.

5 Marius Bewley saw Harvey Birch as Cooper's prescient forecast of his alienated relationship to America in the 1830s and 1840s; see also Franklin 27.

6 Railton observes that Cooper learned the lesson well enough to pass it on, though in milder form, to his nephew Richard Cooper in an 1831 letter (43; 2: 86).

7 Railton reads Cooper's relationship with his mother in classically Freudian terms and consequently gives more emphasis to it (62–69).

8 Cooper's relationship to the De Lanceys was as uncertain as that to his own family. In the early years of his marriage, Cooper composed a genealogy of his wife's family. Though this suggests his desire to identify with the West-chester gentry, it would also have been characteristic of his veiled competitiveness to want to know more about the De Lanceys than did the De Lanceys.

In later life he became embroiled in the De Lanceys' defense, as he did in the defense of his father's land during the Three-Mile Point controversy.

Chapter 4: *The Prairie* and the Family of an Ishmael

1 For Washington's place in American ideology, see Fliegelman's chapter "George Washington and the Reconstituted Family" 197–226; for other literary attempts to meet the problems of the André case, see especially 215–20.

2 Kolodny reads the opening scene as a "grim and succinct summary" of phallic intrusion and rape of the land as Mother (101–02).

3 Though Cooper quite specifically links Boone to Ishmael Bush in this passage, Henry Nash Smith treats the allusion as if it linked Boone and the Leatherstocking (59). This confusion draws attention to the underlying similarities of Cooper's two frontiersmen, akin to the fundamental historical alliance between Judge Temple and Billy Kirby that transcends their opposed attitudes toward nature. Natty and Ishmael are alike forerunners of the white migration.

4 Here I cite the Revised Standard Edition, which translates the passage more emphatically than the King James.

Chapter 5: *Satanstoe*

1 John James Audubon, among other writers, observed that the rapidity of change gave to a country unrelentingly occupied with the real and the practical a paradoxical aura of unreality: "when I remember that these extraordinary changes have all taken place in the short period of twenty years, I pause, wonder, and, although I know all to be a fact, can scarcely believe its reality" (*Delineations of American Scenery and Character,* ed. Francis Hobart Herrick [New York: G. A. Baker, 1926] 4; qtd. in Kolodny 76).

2 A geographically schematic representation of the self's connection with the world as six concentric circles (unearthed by Fliegelman) appeared in an issue of *The Columbian Magazine* of 1789, the year of Cooper's birth. It began with the first sphere around the self and moved outward: "The center circle is 'Self-love Reflected – Family'; [the next,] 'Public Spirit – city, village, township or country'; 'Patriotism – nations of the same religion'; 'Imperfect Philanthropy – nations of the same color'; [and so to] 'Christian charity or Perfect Philanthropy, constituting the Duty, Interest, and Supreme Happiness of Man – the whole world' " (228).

Chapter 6: The Patriarch as Isolato

1 Dekker 249; Franklin puts forward an important caveat against reductively labeling creativity as wish-fulfillment. Cooper is, after all, working here in Poirier's tradition of imagining a world elsewhere to displace temporarily a hostile environment. Yet the way *The Crater* slides from wonderful, imaginative self-sufficiency into dreadful violence makes the issue of the compulsion to control important even in the lovely meditative passages at the center of the book.

2   Shubrick was one of Cooper's most intimate friends. This particular exchange ran from August 1845 through May 1848 (5: 24, 50–53, 74–5, 117–24, 185–94, 204–09, 236–41, 265–68).

3   For an account of the controversy, see *Letters* 3: 271–72; Dekker 153–54; Grossman 106–07.

Works Cited

Adams, Charles Francis. *Familiar Letters of John Adams*. New York: 1876.

"Hutchinson's Third Volume." *North American Review* 38 (Jan. 1834): 134–58.

Beard, James Franklin. Historical Introduction. *The Last of the Mohicans; A Narrative of 1757*. By James Fenimore Cooper. Albany: State U of New York P, 1983. xv–xlviii.

Bell, Michael Davitt. *Hawthorne and the Historical Romance of New England*. Princeton: Princeton UP, 1971.

Bewley, Marius. *The Eccentric Design: Form in the Classic American Novel*. New York: Columbia UP, 1959.

Butterfield, Lyman G. "Cooper's Inheritance: The Otsego County and Its Founders." *James Fenimore Cooper: A Re-Appraisal*. Ed. Mary E. Cunningham. Cooperstown: New York State Historical Assoc., 1954.

Commager, Henry Steele. *Documents of American History*. 9th ed. Englewood Cliffs, N.J.: Prentice-Hall, 1973.

Cooper, James Fenimore. *The American Democrat*. 1838. N.p.: Minerva-Funk, 1969.

Cooper's Works. New Edition. New York: Stringer and Townsend, 1857.

The Letters and Journals of James Fenimore Cooper. Ed. James Franklin Beard. 6 vols. Cambridge, Mass.: Belknap Press of Harvard U, 1960–68.

The Pilot: A Tale of The Sea. New York: Appleton, 1883.

The Pioneers. Ed. James Franklin Beard. Albany: State U of New York P, 1980.

The Wept of Wish-Ton-Wish. Ed. Richard Beale Davis. Columbus, Ohio: Charles E. Merrill, 1970.

Cooper, Susan Fenimore.   *Pages and Pictures, from the Writings of James Fenimore Cooper, with Notes.* New York: W. A. Townsend, 1861.

"Small Family Memories." *Correspondence of James Fenimore Cooper.* Ed. James Fenimore Cooper II. 2 vols. New Haven: Yale UP, 1922.

Cooper, William.   *A Guide to the Wilderness.* Introd. James Fenimore Cooper II. Dublin, 1810. Rochester: n.p., 1897.

Crèvecoeur, St. John de.   *Letters from an American Farmer.* New York: Dutton, 1912.

Dana, Richard Henry, Jr.   *Two Years Before the Mast: A Personal Narrative of Life at Sea.* New York: Penguin, 1981.

Dekker, George.   *James Fenimore Cooper: The American Scott.* New York: Barnes, 1967.

"Sir Walter Scott, the Angel of Hadley, and American Historical Fiction." *American Studies* 17 (1983): 211–27.

Emerson, Ralph Waldo.   *The Complete Works of Ralph Waldo Emerson.* The Centenary Edition. 12 vols. Boston: Houghton, 1903.

Ewart, Mike.   "Cooper and the American Revolution: The Non-fiction." *Journal of American Studies* 11 (1977): 61–80.

Faulkner, William.   *Absalom, Absalom!* New York: Random House, 1936.

Filmer, Sir Robert.   *Patriarcha and Other Political Works of Sir Robert Filmer.* Ed. Peter Laslett. Oxford: Basil Blackwell, 1949.

Fitzhugh, George.   *Cannibals All! or Slaves Without Masters.* Ed. C. Vann Woodward. Cambridge, Mass.: Belknap-Harvard UP, 1960.

Fliegelman, Jay.   *Prodigals and Pilgrims: The American Revolution Against Patriarchal Authority, 1750–1800.* Cambridge: Cambridge UP, 1982.

Forgie, George B.   *Patricide in the House Divided: A Psychological Interpretation of Lincoln and His Age.* New York: Norton, 1979.

Franklin, Wayne.   *The New World of James Fenimore Cooper.* Chicago: U of Chicago P, 1982.

Freneau, Philip.   *The Poems of Philip Freneau, Poet of America.* Ed. Fred Lewis Pattee. Princeton: The University Library, 1902–07.

Fussell, Edwin.   *Frontier: American Literature and the American West.* Princeton: Princeton UP, 1965.

Greven, Philip.   *The Protestant Temperament: Patterns of Child Rearing, Religious Experience, and the Self in Early America.* New York: Knopf, 1977.

Grossman, James.   *James Fenimore Cooper.* New York: W. Sloane, 1949.

Hawthorne, Nathaniel. *The Scarlet Letter*. Eds. Bradley et al. Norton Critical Edition. New York: Norton, 1962.

Heimert, Alan. *Religion and the American Mind from the Great Awakening to the Revolution*. Cambridge, Mass.: Harvard UP, 1966.

Henretta, James A. *The Evolution of American Society, 1700–1815: An Interdisciplinary Analysis*. Lexington, Mass.: D. C. Heath, 1973.

Ironside, Charles Edward. "The Family in Colonial New York: A Sociological Study." Diss. Columbia 1942. New York: n.p., 1942.

Jefferson, Thomas. *Notes on the State of Virginia*. Ed. William Peden. 1785. New York: Norton, 1972.

Jenson, J. Vernon. "British Voices on the Eve of the American Revolution: Trapped by the Family Metaphor." *Quarterly Journal of Speech* 63 (1977): 43–50.

Kaul, A. N. *The American Vision: Actual and Ideal Society in Nineteenth-Century Fiction*. New Haven: Yale UP, 1963.

Keats, John. *Selected Poems and Letters*. Ed. Douglas Bush. Boston: Houghton, 1959.

Kolodny, Annette. *The Lay of the Land: Metaphor as Experience and History in American Life and Letters*. Chapel Hill: U of North Carolina P, 1975.

Lawrence, D. H. *Studies in Classic American Literature*. New York: Viking, 1961.

Lewis, R. W. B. *The American Adam*. Chicago: U of Chicago P, 1955.

Locke, John. *Some Thoughts Concerning Education*. Ed. R. H. Quick. Cambridge: Cambridge UP, 1913.

Lukács, Georg. *The Historical Novel*. Trans. Hannah and Stanley Mitchell. London: Merlin, 1962.

Lyman, Susan E. " 'I Could Write a Better Book than That Myself': Twenty-five Unpublished Letters of James Fenimore Cooper." *The New-York Historical Society Quarterly Bulletin* 29 (1945): 213–39.

McClure, John. *Kipling and Conrad: The Colonial Fiction*. Cambridge, Mass.: Harvard UP, 1981.

McWilliams, John P., Jr. *Political Justice in a Republic: James Fenimore Cooper's America*. Berkeley: U of California P, 1972.

Martin, Wendy. "Woman and the American Revolution." *Early American Literature* 11 (1976–77): 322–35.

Mather, Cotton. *Magnalia Christi Americana*. 2 vols. Hartford: Silas Andrus & Son, 1853.

Melville, Herman.   *Benito Cereno*. Ed. John P. Runden. Lexington, Mass.: Heath, 1965.

Meyers, Marvin.   *The Jacksonian Persuasion: Politics and Belief*. Stanford: Stanford UP, 1957.

Minter, David.   *The Interpreted Design as a Structural Principle in American Prose*. New Haven: Yale UP, 1969.

Molière, Jean Baptiste Poquelin de.   *The Misanthrope* (1666) and *Tartuffe* (1669). Trans. Richard Wilbur. New York: Harvest-Harcourt, 1954.

Morgan, Edmund S.   *The Puritan Family: Religion & Domestic Relations in Seventeenth Century New England*. Revised and enlarged. New York: Harper, 1966.

Nevius, Blake.   *Cooper's Landscapes: An Essay on the Picturesque Vision*. Berkeley: U of California P, 1976.

Paine, Thomas.   *The Rights of Man*. London: Progressive, 1891.

Peck, H. Daniel.   *A World by Itself: The Pastoral Moment in Cooper's Fiction*. New Haven: Yale UP, 1977.

Philbrick, Thomas.   *James Fenimore Cooper and the Development of American Sea Fiction*. Cambridge, Mass.: Harvard UP, 1961.

Pierson, George W.   *Tocqueville and Beaumont in America*. New York: Oxford UP, 1938.

Poirier, Richard.   *A World Elsewhere: The Place of Style in American Literature*. New York: Oxford UP, 1966.

Porte, Joel.   *The Romance in America: Studies in Cooper, Poe, Hawthorne, Melville, and James*. Middletown, Conn.: Wesleyan UP, 1969.

Railton, Stephen.   *Fenimore Cooper: A Study of His Life and Imagination*. Princeton: Princeton UP, 1978.

Ringe, Donald A.   "Cooper's Littlepage Novels: Change and Stability in American Society." *American Literature* 32 (1960): 280–90.

    James Fenimore Cooper. New York: Twayne, 1962.

    The Pictorial Mode: Space and Time in the Art of Bryant, Irving, and Cooper. Lexington: UP of Kentucky, 1971.

Rogin, Michael Paul.   *Fathers & Children: Andrew Jackson and the Subjugation of the American Indian*. New York: Vintage Books, 1975.

Saveth, Edward.   "The Problem of American Family History." *American Quarterly* 21 (1969): 311–29.

Simpson, Lewis P.   "John Adams and Hawthorne: The Fiction of the Real American Revolution." *Studies in the Literary Imagination* 9 (1976): 1–17.

Smith, Henry Nash.   *Virgin Land: The American West as Symbol and Myth*. 1950. Cambridge, Mass.: Harvard UP, 1970.

Spacks, Patricia.   *Imagining a Self: Autobiography and Novel in 18th Century England*. Cambridge, Mass.: Harvard UP, 1976.

Spiller, Robert E.   *Fenimore Cooper: Critic of His Times.* New York: Russell & Russell, 1963.

Sundquist, Eric J.   *Home as Found: Authority and Genealogy in Nineteenth Century American Literature.* Baltimore: Johns Hopkins UP, 1979.

Tocqueville, Alexis de.   *Democracy in America.* Trans. Henry Reeve. Rev. Francis Bowen. Ed. Phillips Bradley. 2 vols. New York: Knopf, 1945.

Tompkins, Jane P.   "No Apology for the Iroquois: A New Way to Read the Leatherstocking Novels." *Criticism* 23 (1981): 24–41.

Turner, Frederick Jackson.   *The Frontier in American History.* New York: Holt, 1962.

Wasserstrom, William.   "Cooper, Freud, and the Origins of Culture." *The American Imago* 17 (1960): 423–37.

Winters, Yvor.   *In Defense of Reason.* Chicago: Swallow Press, 1947.

Wood, Gordon S.   *The Creation of the American Republic: 1776–1787.* Chapel Hill: U of North Carolina P, 1969.

Index